Penang
HERITAGE FOOD

PENANG HERITAGE FOOD

ONG Jin Teong

◇LANDMΔRK◇BOOKS◇

In memory of my mother,

Khoo Chiew Kin,

who started me off on this culinary journey.

CONTENTS

KEY
[F] Finger food
[H] Hawker fare
[D] Dessert / Sweet
[M] Main dish
[O] One-dish meal
[C] Condiment

Planning menus
A home-cooked Nonya meal comprises plain rice served with several main dishes. As with Malay meals, dessert is not normally served. A grand buffet consists of one or more items of finger food, hawker fare, main dishes and desserts.

Note on weights and measures:
5 ml teaspoons and 15 ml tablespoons are used as measures.

Frontispiece: Caricature by Prisca See.

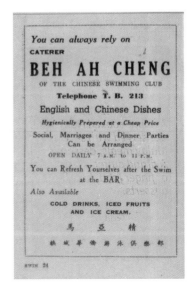

PICTURES OF HERBS AND ASIAN INGREDIENTS

FOREWORD

It is not often that we have a cookbook written by a retired professor in electrical and electronic engineering. Although Dr Ong Jin Teong seems like a newcomer to the food scene, his mother, Khoo Chiew Kin, was well-known in the Penang YWCA and the MGS Old Girls' Association circles. She demonstrated her recipes to the members of the YWCA and the MGS Old Girls in the Fifties, Sixties and Seventies.

Penang Heritage Food is not just about cooking. It is about heritage related to Penang food, giving a new dimension to Penang heritage. It is a well-researched book which gives an insight into the historical background of the dishes, and a personal perspective on how many of the dishes were prepared by Jin Teong's mother, grandmother, aunts, uncles and cousins in their younger days.

This book clearly illustrates the multi-racial and multi-cultural nature of Penang food. Ingredients from many cultures are so well-integrated into the Penang dishes that it is sometimes difficult to work out the origin of a particular dish.

Penang Heritage Food gives a Nonya perspective to Penang food. Hence, there are chapters on the two dominant Malay and Hokkien influences on Penang heritage food as well as Thai and South Indian influences. The latter two distinguishes Penang food from Nonya food found in Melaka and Singapore. The book also gives an insight into the Hainanese and English influences on Penang heritage food.

I wish Jin Teong the best for *Penang Heritage Food* and for his on-going research on Penang heritage food and utensils. I trust that you will enjoy reading and using this book as much as he enjoyed writing it.

LIM GUAN ENG
Chief Minister of Penang

INTRODUCTION

THE IDEA FOR THIS BOOK started when my children, nephews and nieces went abroad for further studies. There was a need to collect well-researched and clearly written recipes for those who already had some exposure to cooking; for others, they had to learn to cook from scratch. Indeed, when my daughter, Clara, was studying in London, I got an urgent email from her asking how to make satay sauce.

My mother, Khoo Chiew Kin, had conducted cooking demonstrations of more exotic dishes for the members of the YWCA and the MGS Old Girls' Association in Penang. My father had compiled these recipes but, unfortunately, the recipes for many everyday, home-cooked dishes had not been recorded. My mother has passed on and there are fewer aunties to ask about cooking, so the recipes and the taste of these dishes will disappear if nothing is done.

Over the years, many of these Penang heritage dishes have been modified so much that what is served today is just a pale image of the original. Older Penangites and the regular visitors to Penang in days gone by will remember, with nostalgia, the taste of food they enjoyed in the Fifties, Sixties, Seventies and maybe even the Eighties.

With the absence of recorded recipes, modifications of family dishes are inevitable due to the preferences and dislikes of members of the household, and hence the original tastes were not faithfully reproduced from one generation to the next. Similarly, for some restaurants, the original recipes and the tastes were not faithfully passed from a retiring chef to his successor. Restaurants and cafés which used to serve good Hainanese food are alas no more! We had the Garden Hotel, Loke Thye Kee at the junction of Penang and Burmah roads, and Wing Loke Café and Kuan Loke Café & Bar, both round the corner from Loke Thye Kee. Hollywood Restaurant still exists, but the food is not up to par.

This book will preserve the Penang heritage food that I grew up with, covering home-cooked food, restaurant and café food, and hawker food. Memories of food cooked by my grandmothers, mother, aunts, uncles and cousins have been recorded, including those for occasions like birthdays, Cheng Beng (a festival remembering the deceased), Nonya weddings and *muah guek* (baby's first month). I have also included details of how the ingredients were prepared.

I recall the restaurant food like Yee Fu Mee and Sar Ho Fun from Foo Heong Restaurant in Cintra Street, the Murtabak and the curries at Meerah and Hamediyah in Campbell Street, and the Hainanese food at Hollywood and Garden Hotel at Tanjong Bungah. We enjoyed the curry puffs and cream puffs from Tip Top at Pulau Tikus and Wing Loke in Penang Road. The stall where one could buy Yee Fu Mee and Sar Ho Fun at the junction of Lorong Selamat and Maclister Road is still there and so is the Bak Moi (pork porridge) stall on Lorong Selamat. I remember these stalls well because I used to live across the road in 63-D Macalister Road, my grandmother's house. There is also a very popular Bak Moi stall at the Kampong Malabar and Penang Road junction where there is also a good Loh Bak (pork roll) and Heh Chnee (prawn fritters) stall.

In the past, Padang Brown during the day and the Esplanade at night were the main hawker centres which served a large variety of food. One *kopi tiam* that was the oasis of Hainanese hawker food was commonly referred to by my family as 'the one next to Queens' (see page 113). It disappeared a long time ago.

Those were the days when the hawkers were mobile, when the food was delivered piping hot to our doorsteps. The various shouts and tok-tok sounds like that of the Wanthan Mee man brings back nostalgic memories. I also remember the Indian man who sold *kuih* and Laksa made by the Nonyas. It is amazing how much these street hawkers could carry as they walked. Up to a few years ago, we could still get Satay Babi grilled outside our house on Thursdays if we were prepared to wait patiently for the satay man. He would even grill the bread that we provided!

Many in today's generation have not taken the trouble to learn how to cook because their parents think they should concentrate on their studies. They can, of course, go back to their mothers for good traditional food, but what about the next generation when mothers becomes grandmothers and mothers cannot cook?

There are not many good published recipes of Penang food. Some recipes are only useful to those who can already cook because the authors have not given details required for beginners. For example, the way ingredients are cut makes a great difference to the dish. Very often, the same ingredients are prepared quite differently for different dishes. Looking at pictures of Nonya dishes in recipe books, suffice to say that the Penang Nonya tradition of finely cutting ingredients is fast disappearing. The vegetables are so *chor* (coarse, in Hokkien), compared to the very fine cutting of the Pai Ti filling prepared by my *luck kim* (sixth aunt) not that many years ago.

Having read many cookbooks, I realise that many of the recipes available do not quite reflect the tastes of the food that I grew up with. I sometimes wonder whether the authors have cooked all the dishes described in their books. Inevitably, there are variations which have evolved from family to family. Some of these variations are mentioned in this book for the benefit of Penang food connoisseurs.

One important objective of this book is to explain the basic cooking techniques of Penang Heritage Food to the uninitiated and to provide simple recipes for home-cook dishes. For the expatriate Malaysian and Singaporean, I share my experience of cooking overseas. In London, where we lived for many years, certain ingredients were not readily available, so local ingredients were substituted. This and other recipe variations are highlighted in this book.

My book is a culinary biography; it is more than just a cookbook. It is also a record of an important aspect of Penang's culture and food heritage. A book about Penang heritage food would inevitably deal with local Penang customs and practices as well as the implements, utensils and crockery used for preparing, cooking, serving and even distributing the food. The *sia nah* (tiered basket), once commonplace, has become an antiquity. Some of the old enamel plates, the batik crockery from China, and Englishware that we used at home are featured here.

Like many Nonyas, my mother and aunties bought Englishware from British departmental stores like Prichards and Whiteaways in Penang and Singapore, and Robinsons in Kuala Lumpur and Singapore. My family still has two sets of the original English crockery which we reserve for use on birthdays and Chinese New Year lunches. Enamel plates and bowls continue to be used today in my mother's house for preparing food.

My mother (third left in the group of ladies) and my father (extreme right with the men) on the breezy balcony of the old Loke Thye Kee restaurant on Penang Road.

PINANG & SIRIH

It is only fitting that pinang (betel nut) and sirih should feature in this book about Penang heritage food. Penang or Pulau Pinang was named after the *Areca catechu* palm that bears areca nuts or *pinang* in Malay – and the tree features prominently in the Penang State flag. Thus, the name 'betel nut' is not strictly correct as the 'betel' refers to the leaf of the betel vine (sirih) although the misnomer highlights the complementary nature of areca nut and sirih. The chewing of betel nut and sirih is an old custom that dates back more than two thousand years.

The betel nut, which grows in a large bunch on the areca palm, turns from green to orange when it ripens. It has a fibrous husk like the coconut but is much smaller. A special hand guillotine called *kacip* in Malay is used to remove the husk and to cut the nut into very thin slices. The intricately decorated *kacip* shown in the photo on the right was used by my grandmother. The sliced betel nuts shown

was sliced using this *kacip*. There are other *kacip* with plain designs and others made of brass; the latter are ornamental as the blades are not functional unless they have separate steel blades attached.

Sirih, the leaf of the betel plant (*Piper betle*), is called lau heok in Penang Hokkien (*heok* means 'leaf') and paan in Indian. It is heart-shaped with visible veins on the glossy leaf. It grows on a vine much like its relative, the pepper plant. There is an area near Pulau Tikus, off Burmah Road and Codrington Avenue called Lau Heok Hnui (hnui being 'estate' in Penang Hokkien).

I can still remember my grandmother chewing betel nut and sirih, often with her friends. It was a way of life which the Nonyas must have adopted from the Malays. I spoke to my elder cousin about her recollection of sirih and she told me that she had part of our grandmother's sirih quid set – unfortunately, most of the set was thrown away because it had deteriorated to such a bad condition. This is the fate of many heritage artefacts as the older generation moves from old houses to new and smaller premises.

To prepare betel nut and sirih for chewing, small amounts of a white and a brownish-red pastes are spread over the sirih leaf. The white paste is *kapur* in Malay or slaked lime or calcium hydroxide while the brownish-red paste is *kapur* mixed with gambier. That is how gambier is added to the sirih in my maternal grandmother's Nonya household. Next, thinly sliced betel nut and a bit of gambier are added onto the leaf which is folded into a triangle.

The package, called the betel quid, is put in the mouth and chewed slowly. After some time the red residue is spat out. This explains why spittoons were strategically placed in houses in the past. They were also very common in coffee shops and even in cinemas, provided in the interest of hygiene and for convenience. For those not familiar with this vessel, a spittoon or *thum phui* is a container, usually of enamel, with a large opening and shaped like a vase with a waist.

According to Malay tradition, the white of the *kapur* signifies purity of the heart. There are tiny spoons specially made for spreading the *kapur*. I came across a collection of them in my mother-in-law's house. Gambier is normally used for curing leather. The Indians in Malaya included other spices in their sirih.

The chewing of betel nut and sirih is bound up with Malay, Penang Hokkien and Indian rituals related to courtship, marriage and sexual relationships between men and women. In Malay culture, sirih is used to describe a young girl who is eligible for marriage. Pinang is the root for several words associated with marriage and courtship, like *pinangan*, which means 'betrothal', and *meminang*, which means 'to ask in marriage'. In the latter, by Malay grammar, the 'p' in *pinang* is replaced by '*mem*' to form a verb.

It is a traditional practice among Nonya parents to personally visit their relatives and friends to invite them for their son or daughter's wedding. This practice is called *pung thiap* (drop invitation) in Penang Hokkien or *pung lau heok* (drop sirih leaf). It goes to show how closely the Nonya and Malay cultures are intertwined.

Betel chewing is prevalent over a large geographical area covering the islands in the Indian and the Pacific Oceans, excluding the Americas. In the past, the habit was as prevalent as cigarette smoking is today. In Taiwan, scantily clad girls still sell betel nuts from roadside stalls all over Taipei.

The ingredients and the tools for preparing the betel quid are arranged in a sirih set or betel quid box. Known as *tepak sirih* in Malay, they come in all shapes and sizes. *Tepak sirih* used to play an important part in conversations, negotiations and important ceremonies at different levels of Malay society – at the royal courts, in villages and the homes of ordinary folk. A *tepak sireh*, representing the important symbols of diplomacy, dialogue, friendship and cooperation, was presented to the United Nations by Malaysia in 2003.

PENANG SPECIALTIES

I HAVE MADE A LIST OF FOOD I consider to be Penang specialities – the food that comes to mind when Penang is mentioned, the food that will bring you back if you are visiting Penang. For the true-blue Penangite, it is the food you will miss when you have been away from Penang for too long.

Tau Sar Pneah

Ask a Penangite what gift of food he would bring to his overseas friends or ask an expatriate what he would take home to give his family a taste of Penang and the answer would likely be Tau Sar Pneah. The best Tau Sar Pneah comes from Penang. The smaller version, known as Tambun Pneah, originated from Tambun, a small town in Seberang Perai (formerly Province Wellesley) across the Straits of Penang, where many shops sold the pastry. Most Penangites associate Tau Sar Pneah with Ghee Hiang, the famous 154-year-old shop. They claim that the taste of their Tau Sar Pneah comes from a secret recipe from Fujian, China, handed down by their forefathers.

Tau Sar Pneah, translated from Hokkien, is 'bean paste biscuit' with the filling being a green bean (mung bean) paste. Those with a discerning palate will be able to taste the fried shallots that give the filling its exquisite flavour. Other ingredients are lard, sugar and salt. More recently, the lard has been replaced to ensure that the biscuit is *halal* and to increase its shelf life. A thin, fluffy multi-layered pastry, which encloses the filling, is glazed and then baked till golden brown.

Tau Sar Pneah are dome-shaped, although a competitor of Ghee Hiang in Chulia Street call their version Dragon Balls – a rather witty brand name. They have also been described as button-shaped, which takes us back to the years when Tau Sar Pneah in Ghee Hiang were stacked and wrapped in grease-proof paper with different coloured labels. Those were the days when we had a choice of *tnee* (sweet) or *kiam* (salty) Tau Sar Pneah. If I am not mistaken, the red label was the sweet variety and the blue label, the salty variety. What we have today is the salty version. Tau Sar Pneah wrapped in grease proof paper is still sold at a shop in Kuantan Road.

The fillings of yesteryear were more moist and, because of that, the shelf life of the pastry was rather short. As the demand was high at Ghee Hiang, we had to place orders way in advance or beg them to sell us a small quantity. This explains the birth of competitors like Cheong Kim Chuan, Him Heang, Dragon Balls and many other Tau Sar Pneah shops along Penang Road, in Chowrasta Market and at Concord in Tanjung Bungah. The good thing is that we now have more choice. Of course we can also get into long arguments as to who makes the best Tau Sar Pneah.

Besides Tau Sar Pneah, these bakeries make other confectioneries such as Phong Pneah, Beh Teh Saw and Hneoh Pneah. Phong Pneah (*phong* is 'puff' in Hokkien) has a spiral puff pastry which is more flaky than that of Tau Sar Pneah. It is flattish, larger than Tau Sar Pneah and the filling is pure-white melted sugar. The Cantonese equivalent is Low Por Pheng, literally, 'wife's biscuit' in that dialect. Beh Teh Saw (translated 'horse hoof crunchy' from Hokkien) is smaller than Phong Pneah and has a filling of molasses and sesame seeds. Hneoh Pneah (*hneoh* is 'joss-stick' in Hokkien and also means 'fragrant') has a thicker and less flaky pastry than Tau Sar Pneah with a drier filling of melted brown sugar mixed with some flour.

Ghee Hiang is also well known for its teel seed or sesame oil which is extracted from roasted sesame seeds. Sesame oil is traditionally used in preparing confinement food specially cooked for Chinese mothers during the first month after giving birth. This could possibly explain why Ghee Hiang's logo features a baby. Recent studies suggest that sesame oil is rich in minerals like calcium, vitamins and anti-oxidants like Omega 6. A dash of sesame oil gives many dishes, including Kay Moi (chicken porridge) and Chee Cheong Fun their special flavour.

Nutmeg

The nutmeg tree (*Myristica fragrans*) was first brought to Penang by the East India Company from what is now the Maluku archipelago in Indonesia; Banda Island was then the centre of nutmeg production. Nutmeg (lau hau in Hokkien or buah pala in Malay) is grown in the Balik Pulau area, which is in central Penang, and also in the north west. Today, the best nutmegs in the world come from Penang.

From the 14th to 19th century, the countries of the world measured political and commercial strength by who controlled the trade of spices, including nutmeg. In the 14th century, one pound of nutmeg in England had a value equivalent to three sheep. Indeed, nutmegs were carried around to flaunt wealth. The rich also carried with them tiny graters, often made of precious metals and of intricate design, to grate their own nutmeg in fashionable restaurants. The high value of nutmeg could explain how nutmeg features in an old English nursery rhyme that we used to recite:

I have a little nut tree,
Nothing would it bear,
But a silver nutmeg,
and a golden pear.

The king of Spain's daughter
came to visit me,
And all for the sake
of my little nut tree.

The nutmeg has three important parts – the outer flesh (the pericarp), the seed (commonly referred to as the nutmeg), and the mace, which is the lacy bright red arillus which covers the seed. The oil obtained from the distillation of ground nutmeg is commercially employed in pharmaceutical (e.g. cough syrup), cosmetic (e.g. toothpaste) and perfume products. Numerous components of the oil are used as natural flavourings in baked food, beverages and sweets. The secret recipe for Coca Cola includes nutmeg oil.

In Penang, we are more familiar with the pale yellow fruit, the outer part of the nutmeg or *lau hau phoey* in Hokkien, which is pickled or candied as snacks. For this purpose, the fruit is cut into various shapes, sizes and forms. The most common has it cut into sixths. In one snack, half of the fruit is thinly sliced in such a way that its shape is kept intact. In another form, the skin is removed and the fruit is pickled in kiam choe (liquorice). The grated or julliene cut version, which is known as *lau hau see*, comes in two versions – heavily coated with sugar or plain.

Boiling the nutmeg flesh with rock sugar produces nutmeg syrup. The syrup, mixed with water, gives a refreshing drink. *Lau hau phoey*, chopped into small pieces, is one of the ingredients of suji (semolina) cake.

Mace is also one of the many powdered spices used in suji cake. Lau hau hwa is what we call mace in Hokkien; *hwa* means 'flower', and is clearly a misnomer. The colour of mace fades from bright red to brownish orange when flattened and dried in the sun, and it is this sunning that develops the intense aroma of the spice. Mace is more commonly available as a ground product. It is widely used in western baked foods, desserts, drinks and savoury dishes; it enhances beverages, soups, meats, stews and sauces. Mace and nutmeg have a similar taste and may be used interchangeably; however, mace has a more delicate, sweeter flavour and is used in light coloured dishes because of the saffron-like colour it imparts.

Lau hau chee, the seed of the nutmeg, is oval and about three centimetres long. It is shiny, dark brown when fresh and lightens and losses its shine with age. When the seed dries, the kernel separates from the shell. Nutmeg seeds should be freshly grated for cooking; ground nutmeg quickly loses the oils that give its flavour.

Nutmeg is mainly used in sweets in Indian cuisine and is an essential ingredient in the classic Indian spice mixture – garam masala. In European cooking, nutmeg and mace are used in many meat and potato dishes, and is a traditional ingredient in mulled wine and mulled cider. The secret ingredient of Penang Nonya Kiam Chai Ark (Salted Vegetable and Duck Soup) is nutmeg; its nutmeg flavour distinguishes it from the Malacca and Singapore versions of the soup.

Nutmeg Preserve & Syrup

This simple recipe for preparing nutmeg syrup is from Andrew Choo who grew up in his family orchard in Balik Pulau. Durians, rambutans, mangosteens, nutmegs and many other fruit are grown there. He explained how nutmeg syrup is made. Only the flesh of the nutmeg is used. There is also another useful by-product of this recipe – nutmeg preserve.

1 kg nutmeg fruit
1 kg rock sugar

Remove the seeds from the nutmeg and set aside for other uses. Wash and split the fruit into four.

To make nutmeg syrup, put the nutmeg into a slow cooker and place rock-sugar on top. Put on slow heat overnight. You can start the process about 10 pm and by morning, the rock sugar would have melted into a syrup. This recipe yields about 750 ml of syrup. Remove nutmeg pieces, dry in the sun and enjoy as preserved nutmeg.

Durians grow directly from the branches of the tree.

Tau Sar Pneah traditionally packed and wrapped in a roll.

The flesh of the nutmeg, lau hau phoey, is cut into various shapes and sizes, and also pickled.

Durian

The durian (*Durio ziberthinus*) is a large, thorny fruit which got its name from *duri*, the Malay word for thorns. It is described as the King of Fruits in Malaysia and Singapore.

Durians are grown on hill slopes on the Western and central regions of Penang, especially around Balik Pulau. The varieties found there are as exotic as they are famous. They include Ang Hae, Musang King, Halia Kuning, Hor Lor and Kor Buay (bitter aftertaste). There is even a bitter-sweet variety named after Lin Feng Chiao (aka Mrs Jackie Chan).

Before the road through the centre of Penang Island linking Ayer Itam to Balik Pulau was built, the sole vehicular access to Balik Pualu was by the round island route. From Georgetown, we could take the North coastal road through Tanjung Bunga and Batu Ferringhi. There are numerous durian orchards after Telok Bahang all the way along the winding road to Balik Pulau. This area is known as Sungei Pinang and our family used to go for picnics by the waterfall there. Unfortunately, the waterfall no longer exists because the stream has been diverted.

One can also go to Balik Pulau in the clockwise direction towards the Bayan Lepas airport from Georgetown. There is a stretch of winding road well after Bayan Lepas. You will see durian trees on both sides of the road. I can remember the nets placed under the trees presumably to prevent the durians from falling on cars and passerbys. We used to hike from the Ayer Itam dam across the centre of Penang to Balik Pulau. We would venture through orchards with durian, clove, nutmeg and other fruit trees. Apparaently, there is an unspoken practise where one can eat the durians that fall on the ground but one cannot take them out of the orchard.

The flower, and hence the fruit, grow from the branches of the durian tree. While running under some durian trees near Murnane reservoir recently, I noticed a lot of flowers on the ground. When I looked up at the tree, I saw monkeys and squirrels. Durian flowers can be eaten raw as *ulam* or stirred fried. So, the flowers are not just enjoyed by monkeys and squirrels but by us humans as well!

When the durian is ripe, the seeds – contained in five segments of the fruit – are covered with custard-like flesh. There could be one or more seeds in each segment, and the prized durians have very small seeds and extremely thick flesh. In the past, to get to the flesh, durian sellers would use a wooden spatula-shaped tool to pry the thorny fruit open. Now they use knives for prying. Durians seeds, like those of chempedak (jackfruit), can be eaten if boiled or roasted.

Ripe durian has a strong odour, much appreciated by the locals, an acquired taste for some foreigners, and considered offensive by others. It has been described in a book on tropical gardening as "French custard passed through a sewage pipe." On the other hand, Alfred Russel Wallace, the co-proponent of the theory of evolution, waxed lyrical about the fruit: "A rich custard highly flavoured with almonds gives the best general idea of it, but there are occasional wafts of flavour that call to mind cream-cheese, onion-sauce, sherry-wine, and other incongruous dishes. Then there is a rich glutinous smoothness in the pulp which nothing else possesses, but which adds to its delicacy. It is neither acid nor sweet nor juicy; yet it wants neither of these qualities, for it is in itself perfect. It produces no nausea or other bad effect, and the more you eat of it the less you feel inclined to stop. In fact, to eat Durians is a new sensation worth a voyage to the East to experience." My elder children who grew up in London wouldn't touch durian even with a barge pole, but my youngest child who grew up in Singapore loves it!

Ripe durians have a short shelf-life. Hence, in the old days, durian flesh was made into durian *kuih* (also known as durian cake) before they soured. Durian which were unsellable were also used. Durian *kuih* making is a Penang cottage industry especially in the durian-growing areas of Balik Pulau and Sungei Pinang. In the past, we learnt through word of mouth where we could buy good durian *kuih*. It is only in more recent times that they are marketed commercially in Penang, although many Penangite still prefer the home-made variety. There are versions of durian *kuih* in Perak and

East Kalimantan known as Lempok Durian. A variety of durian *kuih* is also commercially available in Thailand.

The process of making durian *kuih* is time-consuming and rather tedious. The flesh is removed from the seeds and passed through a sieve to obtain a fine texture. It is then cooked over a slow fire, traditionally in a large brass pan. It must be continuously stirred with a large wooden stirrer to ensure that the durian does not stick to the pan. When oil appears, sugar is added and the mixture is continuously stirred till it turns brown or nearly black and sticky. The process takes several hours. Some cooked and mashed durian flesh is finally added to the mixture to make the durian *kuih* oily and shiny, and also to add bulk. The mixture is then divided into portions and kneaded into balls. To obtain an elastic consistency, each portion is thrown onto the work-top a couple of times. They are then rolled into cylindrical shapes of about 3 cm in diameter and wrapped up in plastic sheets.

Ngoh Hiang Hoon - Five Spice Powder

'Five fragrance powder' is the literal translation from Hokkien for ngoh hiang hoon. Traditionally, ngoh hiang hoon, which looks very much like cocoa powder, is made up of five spices: cloves, cinnamon, star anise, fennel seeds and Sichuan pepper. Five is the number of elements which is central to Chinese philosophy. The elements wood, fire, earth, metal and water are associated with a corresponding taste: sour, bitter, sweet, spicy and salty. Five Spice Power, having nutritional and curative benefits, is part of Chinese traditional medicine where the line between food and medicine is blurred. That is why ngoh hiang hoon is traditionally prepared and sold by Chinese medical halls. Incidentally, star anise, which is one of the five spices, is a key ingredient in the manufacture of the anti-flu drug, Tamiflu.

Five Spice Powder is used for marinating meats for grilling, frying or roasting, and is used liberally in the preparation of roast duck and grilled ribs. It gives a special flavour to the sauce (*lor*) served with Lor Mee. *Lor* is also one of the dipping sauces that goes with a Penang Hokkien dish called Lor Bak (see page 93). It gives a distinct and interesting flavour to different foods like Cantonese dumpling (Hum Yok Chong) and flatcake (Hum Cheen Pieng). As much as a doughnut connoisseur would say that doughnuts don't taste the same without nutmeg, so Hum Cheen Pieng would not taste the same to a Penangite without ngoh hiang hoon.

Ngoh hiang hoon from Penang is very fragrant and only a small quantity is needed. When I was in London, my cousin brought me a large packet from Kuala Lumpur. It was rather coarsely ground and I had to use a larger quantity to obtain the same flavour. If you look at the ingredients of some commercial Five Spice Powders, you will find also pepper, nutmeg, dried orange peel, coriander seeds and rice.

The ngoh hiang hoon that I use is much better than the supermarket variety. I buy it from the Pok Oy Thong (P.O.T.) Medical Hall in Chulia Street, whose proprietor is Liew Kwong Fatt. His grandfather, Liew Kwai Sang, started the business in the late 18th century. Pok Oy Thong ngoh hiang hoon is much costlier than regular brands.

Heh Ko - Prawn Paste

Heh ko, known as petis udang in Malay, is a thick, black prawn paste that originates from Penang. It looks very similar to Marmite – the thick dark brown food spread familiar to those living in the United Kingom and many Commonwealth countries. However, that is where the similarity ends, as heh ko has a unique taste and smell.

In Asian food culture, every part of a food product is used. This approach applies to prawns in the manufacture of heh ko. The prawn shells, especially the heads, are boiled with salt into a stock. The stock is concentrated and caramelized sugar is added to give it a dark colouring. Flour is then added to thicken it into a gooey paste. That is why the Malays also refer to heh ko as *otak udang* which means 'brains of the prawn'.

Heh ko is normally diluted with water and used as a condiment; it then looks dark grey. It is commonly served with Penang Laksa, both the *assam* and *lemak* varieties. The addition of heh ko distinguishes Penang Laksa from other types of Laksa. It is also indispensable in Penang Rojak – a fruit and vegetable salad which has other ingredients such as powdered belacan and pounded peanuts. Chee Cheong Fun in Penang is also served with heh ko, sweet sauce (tnee cheow) and chilli sauce.

Tanau Kiam Hu - Mergui or Dried Salted Ikan Kurau

Another food produce expatriate Penangites buy when they return to Penang is tanau kiam hu – the dried salted Ikan Kurau (Giant Threadfin) also referred to as Mergui dried fish. Kiam hu is 'salt fish' in Hokkien. It used to be imported from Mergui in Burma, a busy port in the Mergui archipelago west of the Isthumus of Kra, north of Phuket. The Mergui Archipelago is part of the Tanintharyi Division of Burma, better known by its old name, Tenasserim. The term 'tanau' in tanau kiam hu could be a Hokkien corrupted abbreviation for Tenasserim.

Tanau kiam hu comes in large flat pieces about 1 to 1.5 cm thick and about 40 cm long. Each piece is sliced from an Ikan Kurau to remove the vertebra. The best part of the preserved fish is the portion in the middle between the stomach and the tail. Kiam hu kut, the bones (*kut*) of the salt fish are sold separately. These bones give flavour to various dishes like Salt Fish Bone Curry, Tow Fu Soup and Kiam Hu Pork. One distinct characteristic of tanau kiam hu is that it is not as salty as other salt fish, and the texture is crumbly even after it has been fried. Fried tanau kiam hu is a standard garnish for Penang dishes like Curry Kapitan. It also goes very well with rice porridge and salted duck egg. Salt fish gives its special flavour to other Penang dishes like steamed pork, fried beansprouts, Kiam Hu Rice (similar to claypot rice, this was a dish cooked and served at our family picnics at Telok Bahang) and Kiam Hu Branda (a spicy salt fish dish). Beansprouts, which normally taste rather bland, are brought to life when fried with kiam hu.

When deep-fried in oil, tanau kiam hu gives out a lovely fragrance to those who appreciate it. Hence, frying it overseas could create a bit of a problem as the smell waft across to the neighbours. Luckily it smells a bit like burnt cheese, so this is our standard excuse if there are any complaints from next door!

Kiam hu is now a luxury item; a piece the size of ones palm could cost as much as RM50! The cost is likely to go up since many of the fish are frozen and exported. Processing kiam hu is also tedious and time consuming.

Belacan - Dried Shrimp Paste

Belacan is made from fermented shrimp or eu heh in Hokkien – literally translated, it means 'tiny shrimp'. These shrimps are less than one centimeter in length. The fresh shrimp, which are white with a pink tinge, are salted, spread out in trays and allowed to ferment under the hot sun. After several days of fermentation, they disintegrate and the colour changes to a dark purplish brown, by which time the shrimp stick together to form a pulp. The pulp is mashed in a grinder or pounded and then compacted in wooden vats where it is allowed to further ferment for many days before being spread out to dry for several more hours. This fermentation and drying cycle is repeated until mature belacan is ready to be fashioned into the blocks that we buy.

Similar products are made in Malacca and countries like Thailand (gkapbi), Indonesia (terasi) and Phillipines (bagoong alamang). The manufacturing process varies from country to country and even from region to region depending on the type of shrimp used. The process of making belacan in Malacca is simpler than in Penang which results in belacan that is

When one buys five spice powder in Penang, the shopkeeper will ask whether you want the higher quality powder which costs more!

Heh ko (shrimp paste) distinguishes Penang Laksa from versions of Laska found elsewhere.

Belacan is traditionally fashioned into blocks. It is a key ingredient in Malay and Nonya cuisine.

not as well fermented as the Penang variety. My cousin has a mother from Penang and a mother-in-law from Malacca. One says Penang belacan is better while the other maintains that Malaccan belacan is the superior one. I don't have this problem; my mother-in-law, like my mother, is from Penang and I think the best belacan comes from Penang.

Belacan is an indispensable ingredient in Malaysian cuisine and without it Malay and Nonya cooking would be very different. It is used in Sambal Belacan (see page 39), an important condiment used by the Malays and Nonyas, as well as in many curries like Ikan Assam Pedas, Curry Kapitan, Assam Laksa and Laksa Lemak. Belacan, when toasted and pounded, gives Penang Rojak its special taste and flavour.

For those not so familiar with this condiment, the smell of belacan may be repulsive, However, good quality belacan from Penang has a nice aroma similar to that of blue cheeses. In Nonya cooking, belacan is sliced into thin pieces and toasted. The smell of toasted belacan is not as strong and is more pleasant. Still, for this reason, belacan has earned a place in the list of Weird Food on the Internet. The website offers the following advice when cooking with belacan, "You want to make sure you seal off the kitchen from other parts of the house. The smell is VERY potent". Those of us who have toasted belacan while living overseas will understand this problem!

PENANG LAKSA AND OTHER LAKSA

Penang Laksa
In Penang, when we talk about our Laksa, we are referring to Assam Laksa – a spicy hot and sour fish soup poured over rice noodle with garnishes of finely shredded cucumber, lettuce, onions, pineapple, bunga kantan (bud of torch ginger), chillies and mint. *Assam* is a Malay word meaning 'sour'. It could also refer to tamarind, although some varieties of tamarind – like the Thai variety – are sweet.

Penang Assam Laksa uses coarse bee hoon (rice noodles). Today, the noodles used are made commercially or reconstituted from dried bee hoon. In the old days, the *laksa bor* – *bor* means 'mould' in Hokkien – was made from scratch from uncooked rice grains. The rice was first ground in a granite grinder called *cheok bo*. Water was added in the grinding process and the ground rice was collected in a muslin bag and hung up to allow the water to drain away. Part of the drained ground rice was mixed with water and cooked to obtain the *ibu* or 'mother' in Malay and Penang Hokkien. The rest was mixed with lek thau hoon (ground mung beans) and kneaded with the *ibu* into a dough. The mung beans made the *laksa bor* have a *khiew* or *al dente* texture. The dough was put into a hand press which squeezed out long threads of bee hoon.

The noodles went straight into a pot of boiling water and was plunged in cold water when cooked. Skeins of the noodles were then drained on a large, woven bamboo tray or *nyiru*, covered with muslin cloth. In Thailand, *laksa bor* is called *jap*, which means 'to catch'. It describes how you have to dip your hand into the cold water to catch a portion of the bee hoon and then twirl them into shape. I can still remember how it was done at my grandmother's house in Tanjong Tokong.

In the old days, the amount of Laksa eaten is measured by the number of *laksa bor*. We would say, "I cannot eat any more as I had six *bor* of Laksa!" A bowl of Laksa would normally have one or two *bor*.

Nonya Kuih Laksa
There were Nonyas who made Nonya *kuih* (sweets/dessert) and Laksa at home. The food was carried and sold all over Georgetown by Indian *kuih* men. Unfortunately, there are very few of the *kuih* men, if any, left today. There was one

based at the back of Penang Plaza and another one at the market at Mount Eskine near Fettes Park. The Laksa they sold had a very distinctive taste. It was probably due to the bunga kantan cooked in with the gravy. Normally, sliced bunga kantan is added as a garnish and not cooked together with the soup for Nonya Laksa.

Malay Laksa

My father's family lived in the middle of a Malay kampong in Tanjong Tokong. When we were young, we spent most of our Sundays at the Penang Chinese Swimming Club nearby as most of my uncles and aunties had very close links with the club. There used to be a Malay hawker selling Assam Laksa and roast cuttlefish there. This Malay Laksa is a simpler version of Penang Assam Laksa – probably closer to Kedah Laksa. The soup is clearer and less chilli red.

Laksa Lemak

Laksa Lemak (see page 179) is sometimes referred to as Siamese Laksa. *Lemak*, in Malay, means 'creamy' referring to the creaminess of the coconut milk added to the soup which, unlike Penang Assam Laksa, is not sour.

Curry Mee

Curry Mee is similar to the Laksa of both Kuala Lumpur and Singapore, both of which are coconut-milk based. *Mee* (fresh yellow noodles) and/or bee hoon (rice vermicelli) and beansprouts are served with the Curry Mee soup. The Penang version is less creamy and has tow pok (soya bean puff), hum (cockles), huet (coagulated blood) and soft ju hu (cuttlefish). Unlike the Singapore variety, it is not served with sliced *Polygonum* (chien hom or kesom). Serai (lemongrass) is what gives Penang Curry Mee its distinct flavour. There is a version of Curry Mee from Kuala Lumpur that is served with chicken.

Laksa from elsewhere

The other states of Malaysia also have their own Laksa. The versions from Kedah and Perlis are sour, but those from Johor, Kelantan, Melaka, Pahang and Sarawak are both *lemak* and sour, often using assam gelugor, a sour fruit. The Laksa from Malaysia are generally fish-based except for Melaka Laksa which is prawn-based.

There is a Burmese noodle dish, Mohinga, which is similar to Laksa Lemak. In my student days in the early Sixties, I used to patronize a Burmese restaurant run by a Burmese widow near Tottenham Court Road in London. It served something close to Penang Laksa Lemak. At about the same time, I first tasted Singapore Laksa at a Singapore restaurant at Kensington. The nearest food to it, according to my Penang palate, was Curry Mee. I wondered why it was called Laksa when it was so apparently different from the Assam Laksa I was familiar with. What did they have in common? I realized that these dishes share some common ingredients like chillies, shallots, lemongrass, turmeric and belacan. The gravies are thus essentially the same. The variations are determined by the meat used, the proportions of the ingredients, and whether the Laksa is *assam* or *lemak*. Key ingredients like limau perut (kaffir lime leaves) for Laksa Lemak and the kesom (*Polygonum*) for Singapore Laksa and Penang Laksa also give each dish its own distinctive flavour. To a certain extent, the garnishes and condiments likewise contribute to the differences.

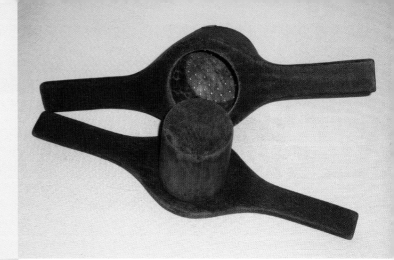

A press used to squeeze out threads of bee hoon to make laksa bor. We kept track of the amount of Laksa we ate by the number of bor we consumed.

In the old days, Nonya Laksa was sold by Indian kuih men who plied their trade around Georgetown.

PENANG LAKSA
ASSAM LAKSA

This Assam Laksa recipe produces my mother's home-cooked version, similar to that served by hawkers in Penang, except that there is more fish. This is the recipe used in her cooking demonstrations to members of the YWCA and to the Penang Methodist Girls' School Old Girls' Association.

Recently, I heard someone complain to a hawker that there wasn't enough fish in her Penang Laksa. Could she have more fish if she was prepared to pay more? What the customer did not know is that in hawker-style Laksa, the fish is all mashed up and it is not easy to separate from the soup. The advantage of cooking your own Laksa is that you can not only have as much fish as you want, but you can also choose the type of fish. Various fish can be used for Laksa: Lait Hu (Ikan Pupu), Ikan Parang (Wolf-herring), Ikan Kembong (Mackeral) and Ikan Terubuk (Shad). Small fish used by hawkers are Chee Ya Hu, which looks like a small Mullet, and small Kembong (Chubb Mackeral). Chee Ya Hu used to be cheap in my youth but it is not so today and it is more labour intensive to remove its tiny bones.

Penang Laksa is a Nonya dish adopted from the Malays; the ingredients are very similar to Ikan Assam Pedas (see page 42). There is another version which I refer to as the Nonya *kuih* version cooked by the Nonyas and sold by the *kuih* man. In this and some other family recipes, sliced bunga kantan (torch ginger bud) is boiled in the Laksa soup.

I find the fresh Laksa bee hoon available in Singapore better than the ones served in Laksa stalls in Penang because they are more *al dente* or *khiew*; the ones from Penang are too soft and tastes like bee thai bak. We used spaghetti or suome, a dried Japanese noodle, when we were in London.

Penang prawn paste, heh ko or petis udang, is added to give Assam Laksa its special taste. Unfortunately, I find that certain stalls spoil their Laksa by adding too much heh ko. *Polygonum* is what gives Assam Laksa its distinctive flavour. In Penang, it is generally not eaten; the leaves and stalks are removed from the soup before serving. Interestingly, chopped up kesom is added as a garnish in Singapore Laksa. Generally, lengkuas (galangal) is not one of the ingredients in Assam Laksa but it is used for Laksa Lemak. Tamarind (assam) is used to give Assam Laksa its sour and sweet taste. Sliced assam phoi (assam gelugor) is also added if the tamarind used is not sour enough.

Most stalls in Georgetown, Ayer Itam and Balik Pulau serve only Assam Laksa. A few serve both Assam Laksa and Laksa Lemak. Generally, the stalls that serve both – like the one at Burma Lane opposite the Pulau Tikus police station – have a strong Thai or Burmese influence. Traditionally, in our family, the *assam* and *lemak* versions are cooked and served together, such that we have difficulty deciding which to eat first. Personally, I start with Laksa Lemak, then the Assam Laksa and then a mixture of both. The last approach may explain why the Laksa from Johor, Kelantan, Melaka and Pahang are both *lemak* and sour. Both Penang Assam Laksa and Laksa Lemak are fish based, but the latter has ingredients like prawns and crabs, depending on each family's recipe. My mother's recipe uses chopped prawns.

Penang Laksa
(Serves 12)

Noodles
1.5 kg fresh bee hoon (thick rice vermicelli)*

Rempah
30 – 35 dried chillies (about 30g)
8 fresh red chillies (about 100g)
2 tbsp belacan
3 cloves garlic
150 g shallots
3 cm x 1.5 cm diameter fresh kunyit (turmeric)
6 stalks serai (lemongrass)

Soup
2 tbsp assam (tamarind), without seeds
3 pieces assam gelugor, more for a more sour taste
1.2 kg fish, including bones
3.5 litres water
6 large stalks of chien hong / kesom (*Polygonum*)
2 tbsp sugar
3 tsp salt

Garnishes
1 cucumber
3 onions (about 150 g)
200 g local lettuce, roots removed
100 g mint leaves
½ small pineapple (about 350 g)
2 bunga kantan (torch ginger buds)
4 fresh chillies
10 keat lah or limau kesturi (calamansi limes)
4 tbsp heh ko (prawn paste)

* Use half the weight if using dried bee hoon.

Rempah (Spice Paste)
Remove the stalks of the dried and fresh chillies, and the seeds too if you prefer your Laksa less spicy. Soak the dried chillies in water for about 15 minutes.

Either slice the belacan thinly or fashion it into a thin wafer; grill or toast till dry and slightly dark brown. Alternatively, use 4 tsp of powdered belacan.

Smash the garlic and remove the skin. Peel the shallots and cut off the root ends. Remove and discard the skin from the kunyit and chop up the kunyit.

Cut off and discard the leafy part of the serai. Use only the white portion of the stalk approximately 5 cm from the root; smash the stalks and slice finely. If you have an abundant supply of serai you can be a bit choosy, but if you are living overseas where serai is more precious, there is no harm using the greener part; it adds bulk to the *rempah*.

Pound or grind all the *rempah* ingredients into a fine paste with a pounder or food processor. Start with the garlic and serai as they are more difficult to grind or pound. If a food processor is used, 100 - 200 ml of water may have to be added to ensure that the *rempah* is ground efficiently.

Laksa Soup
It is better to cook the Laksa soup ahead of time and re-heat before serving.

Soak the tamarind in 100 ml of water. Squeeze the pulp between your fingers. Then use a spoon to pass it through a sieve into a bowl so as to separate the pulp from the fibre. Discard the fibre. Reserve the tamarind liquid.

Remove one or two of the outer petals of the bunga kantan, Slice the bunga kantan stem. Set all aside for boiling with the fish stock.

Boil the water and cook the fish in it. Remove the fish when cooked, allow to cool and separate the flesh from the bones. Set the flesh aside. Return the fish bones and other parts of the fish to the stock and simmer for another 10 - 15 minutes to obtain a better stock.

Heat up the wok or *belanga*. When it is hot, put in the *rempah* and cook for about 4 or 5 minutes without oil until fragrant. Stir continuously to ensure that it does not stick to the wok and add 30 - 50 ml of water if the *rempah* is too dry. Add the fish stock, the tamarind liquid, assam gelugor and the sliced bunga kantan stem and outer petals. Bring to a boil, then lower the heat and simmer for 30 minutes.

Add the fish, chien hong, assam gelugor (if using), salt and sugar and bring to a boil again. Lower heat and simmer for another 15 minutes. The Laksa soup is ready for serving.

Garnishes
Slice the cucumber. Stack slices and cut into thin sticks.

Cut the onions into two from shoot to root, and slice thinly across.

Stack the lettuce leaves and slice into 5 mm strips.

Pluck the mint leaves and discard the stalks.

Skin the pineapple and remove the core of the fruit. Cut the pineapple into sticks of about 5 mm thickness.

Cut the remaining bunga kantan into two, lengthwise, and then slice thinly along the length, starting at the tip of the flower bud until the white stalk of the bud can be seen.

Remove the stalk from the fresh chillies, de-seed (unless you like your Laksa spicy hot) and slice diagonally.

Cut the limes into two and remove the seeds.

Dilute the heh ko with an equal volume of boiled water.

Blanch the fresh bee hoon. If you are using dried bee hoon, soak it in warm water for at least 30 minutes and add to it a generous amount of boiling water. Note that some bee hoon, depending on the quality, will disintegrate if over-boiled.

Assembly
To serve, place a serving of the bee hoon in a bowl, spread the garnishes on top and add the soup. Top with a teaspoon or two of heh ko according to taste and squeeze in the juice from one or two limes depending on how sour a Laksa you prefer.

Two types of assam: tamarind or assam (back) and assam gelugor or assam phoi (front).

CHAR KOAY TEOW

Char Koay Teow is a Teowchew and Hokkien hawker food. *Char* means 'fried' in Penang Hokkien and koay teow is flat rice noodles. In Penang, koay teow is fried with beansprouts, prawns and other garnishes. Penang Char Koay Teow is distinct from that served in other parts of Malaysia or Singapore. What is special about the Char Koay Teow from Penang is that it includes fresh prawns and cockles, bak eu pok (fried lard cubes), ku chai (chives) and sliced lap cheong (Chinese sausages). Invariably, it is fried individually in a very hot pan.

Traditionally, duck egg is used instead of chicken egg which is normally used in most stalls today. Duck egg is creamier but, unfortunately, more sinful in terms of cholesterol. There are still a few stalls that use duck egg – like the one at the junction of Malay Street and Carnarvon Street.

The main difference between Penang and Singapore Char Koay Teow is that the Penang version does not have the sweetness from the black sauce and has chives and Chinese sausage. The koay teow used in Penang is also much thinner than that normally available in Singapore. Some market stalls in Singapore do sell the thinner koay teow but you have to specifically ask for it. The koay teow from Ipoh is even thinner. This could be due to the Cantonese influence there. Cantonese ho fun which traditionally comes in sheets and is cut into strips wider than koay teow by the cook, is generally thinner than koay teow. The texture of ho fun and koay teow are also slightly different. To appreciate the difference in texture between koay teow and ho fun, I would like to bring in chee cheong fun – rice sheets – which has the softest texture of the three. Koay teow has a texture that falls between that of chee cheong fun and ho fun.

It is best to use fresh koay teow while it is still soft. If kept in the refrigerator, it hardens and has to be warmed up in a microwave oven or steamed before use. It also doesn't keep for long as it tends to become mouldy. There are some good dried koay teow (described as sha ho fan) from China and Vietnam which can be re-constituted into a very credible fresh koay teow substitute.

I am not one for cockles (hum in Hokkien) with my Char Koay Teow but in the interest of food heritage I have included it in the recipe. Cockles remind me of a well-known Char Koay Teow stall that was once at the junction of Cantonment Road and Gurney Drive. We used to fish there and I remember an area of the beach that was covered with discarded cockle shells. As cockles have a muddy taste when they have just been harvested, they need to be soaked in water to gradually expel the mud. The Char Koay Teow man did this by leaving his cockles in a net bag in the sea. I suggest that it is more convenient to buy cockles which have been shelled.

Take-away Char Koay Teow was traditionally wrapped in a banana leaf placed over a newspaper and tied up into a cone with *kiam chow*, a string made from grass. The take-away fried koay teow took on the flavour of the banana leaf; that is why some stalls still serve their Char Koay Teow on a small square piece of banana leaf today.

A healthier cooking oil like canola can be used to fry Char Koay Teow but, once in a while, it would be nice, though sinful, to add bak eu phok as it is done traditionally. If you want to go the whole hog, you can cook with lard.

The amount of oil used in this recipe is kept to a minimum. Traditionally, more oil is added to prevent the koay teow from sticking to the pan. Here, water is used at different stages of the frying process for the same purpose. A very hot fire is needed to fry Char Koay Teow.

Char Koay Teow
(Serves 4)

400 g fresh koay teow or 200 g dried koay teow
   (flat rice noodles)
20 prawns
8 cloves garlic
240 g beansprouts
40 cockles
80 g Chinese sausage
8 stalks chives
2 tbsp of chilli powder
4 eggs
12 tsp oil
12 tsp light soya sauce
120 ml water, salted with a pinch of salt
Ground pepper
Bak eu phok (fried lard cubes), optional

Divide the ingredients into four equal portions and fry each serving of Char Koay Teow individually.

Fresh koay teow comes in sheets which are stacked and cut into strips. The strips must be separated before frying.

If using dried koay teow, bring to a boil a pot of water sufficient to cover all the dried koay teow. Put the koay teow into the boiling water and turn off the heat before the water boils again. Leave aside. Just before frying, strain the koay teow using a colander and rinse in cold water.

Shell and devein the prawns and rub in a bit of salt. Wash the cockles and pour hot water over them so that the shells open. Remove each cockle with a teaspoon and leave to soak in bit of water.

Smash the garlic with the flat side of a chopper,

remove the skin and chop the garlic finely. Rinse the beansprouts, remove the shells of the beans, if any, and drain the water. Wash the chives, remove any unwanted old leaves and cut the chives into 3 cm lengths.

Slice the Chinese sausage diagonally to about 2 mm thickness.

Mix ½ tbsp of chilli powder with 1 tbsp of water to form a smooth paste

Heat a pan or wok and add 2 tsp of cooking oil only when the pan is hot. Spread the oil over the pan or wok, then add the chopped garlic and stir continuously.

Before the garlic turns brown, add the prawns and fry till they turn white or red, depending on the type of prawns used. Add the chilli paste and stir quickly.

Now add the koay teow and 2 tsp of the light soya sauce. Stir well for about 2 minutes. Add about 1 tbsp of the salted water if the koay teow sticks to the pan.

Include the beansprouts and continue to stir fry. Add the sliced sausages and mix well with the other ingredients. Add another tablespoon of salted water if too dry.

Make a well in the middle of the wok by moving the contents to the sides. Add 1 tsp of oil and break in an egg. Add 1 tsp of light soya sauce and ground pepper. Partially scramble the egg and, when it is half cooked, mix it with the koay teow.

Add the chives and cockles and give a good final stir before turning off the fire. If the koay teow is stuck to the pan, cover the pan and leave awhile so that the steam will soften and separate the bits that are stuck.

A very hot pan is what is needed for frying char koay teow so that the dish acquires the 'breath' of the wok. In Penang, this dish is fried in individual portions so that the cooking can be done at optimum heat.

HOKKIEN MEE

Penang Hokkien Mee is a prawn-based soup served with mee (fresh yellow noodles) and/or bee hoon (rice vermicelli), beansprouts and kangkong (water convolvulous). It is topped with sliced prawns and thinly sliced pork. It is the stock, made with the inclusion of the shells and heads of prawns, which gives the soup its distinct taste. There are two other garnishes, besides a blob of plain chilli paste, that give the Hokkien Mee its special flavour – the eu chang (fried sliced shallots) and fried lard cubes (bak eu phok).

Traditionally, Penang hawker food is not served with much meat because of its cost. This home-cooked version has more *leow* (ingredients), including pork ribs, compared to the hawker version.

The secret of a good Hokkien Mee soup is a good stock made from pork bones. It is best to prepare the soup the day before or in the morning for serving later in the day. Spare ribs are traditionally used for home-made Hokkien Mee. There are two types – bak kut (back bone) and pai kut (ribs). The latter is normally preferred but I find that it could have a lot of fat. I suggest using bones, spare ribs and a lean cut for this recipe. The meat is sliced and served as a garnish but not as thinly sliced as the hawker version from my school days. What do you expect for twenty cents a bowl in the Fifties? Today, it costs RM3.00 or more and the portion is smaller.

How thing have changed! These days, we only get a few token pieces of kangkong and not as much beansprouts as we used to. Both these vegetables were very cheap when I was young; we could ask for free beansprouts when we bought soya bean cake at the market, but today beansprouts cost as much as the noodles. However, now as well as then, you can choose to have the yellow noodles by itself in your Hokkien Mee or combine it with bee hoon to make bee hoon mee – that is how you would order it from the hawker.

Today, some stalls have added boiled eggs to Hokkien Mee. I am not used to this; I like my Hokkien Mee the traditional way – without boiled eggs! A well-known Penang food blogger even mentions boiled egg in her recipe, making it sound like a normal practice.

The fried noodle dish, known as Hokkien Mee in Singapore and Kuala Lumpur is known as Hokkien Char in Penang. Hokkien Char cooked by Penang Hokkiens is not commonly served with Sambal Belacan. However, there is a version cooked by the Penang Hainanese, which is served with it. The Nonya influence predominates in the version from this recipe.

In the old days, hawker food was served in octogonal bowls. They come in various designs of flowers, fruits or roosters. The last is probably more familar. Different hawkers would use different designs to ensure that the bowls were not mixed up. These bowls are still made and used today but they are now round.

Hokkien Mee
(Serves 12)

400 g pork spare ribs (cut into bite-size pieces)
300 g pork bones
400 g prawns
150 g shallots
3 tbsp chilli powder
7 tbsp water
300 g beansprouts
200 g kangkong (water convolvulous), roots removed
300 g lean pork
Salt
Ground pepper
3 tbsp light soya sauce
200 g dried bee hoon (rice vermicelli)
1 kg mee (fresh yellow noodles)
6 tbsp oil
3 tbsp sugar
Bak eu phok (fried lard cubes)

To enjoy the Hokkien Mee from the stall opposite the police station at Pulau Tikus, you have to go early on holiday weekends.

Noodles drying in the sun.

Boil 3 litres of water in a large pot. Add the bones, spare ribs and bring to a boil again before turning down the heat to low to simmer for at least half an hour.

Remove the heads and the shells of the prawns and keep aside. Devein the prawns, coat them with ½ tsp of salt and leave aside.

Peel the shallots, wash, dry and slice them evenly.

Mix the chilli powder with the 7 tbsp of water into a smooth paste.

Wash the beansprouts and drain. Wash the kangkong, removing the yellow leaves. Cut the stem between the leaves so that each leaf has a bit of the stem attached.

Cut the lean meat into 3 x 3 cm slices and marinate with ½ tsp salt, pepper and 3 tbsp soya sauce.

Soak the bee hoon in warm water for at least ½ hour to separate the strands that are stuck together. Drain and set aside in a colander.

Separate the noodles into two portions for blanching. To blanch one portion of the mee, use a large pot to boil 2.5 litres of water. Disentangle the noodles and put them into the boiling water. Turn off the fire just before the water boils again so as not to overcook the noodles which are already cooked. Transfer into a colander and rinse with cold running water. Drain and keep aside. You can mix in a bit of oil to prevent the noodles from sticking together. Blanch the noodles in batches if a large pot is not available. Repeat for the other portion of the noodles.

To blanch the bee hoon, bring about 2 litres of water in a large pot to a boil and put in the soaked bee hoon. Turn off the heat just before the water boils again. Pour the bee hoon into a colander with a pot below it to collect the hot water, which is to be kept for blanching the beansprouts. Rinse the bee hoon in cold running water and keep aside for serving.

Bring to a boil the hot water used for blanching the bee hoon and put in the beansprouts when it boils. Blanch the beansprouts, remove, rinse in cold water and set aside. Put in the kangkong just before the water boils again. Stir the vegetable briskly and pour into a colander to rinse with cold water. Drain and set aside.

Heat up the 6 tbsp of oil, then add the sliced shallots. Stir continuously and when the onions are nearly golden turn down the fire and move them to the side of the wok to drain. Transfer the fried shallots on to a paper towel to absorb the excess oil.

Fry the chilli paste in the same oil on a low fire until the oil turns red. Remove three-quarters of the fried chilli paste to use as a condiment.

Fry the prawn heads and shells in the chilli paste left in the wok until you can smell the fragrance of the fried prawns. Add 1 litre of water and bring to the boil. Simmer for 10 to 15 minute.

Transfer the prawn heads and shells to a food processor to liquidize. Pour the liquidized prawn heads and shells into the stock pot using a sieve to filter off the shells. Mix the shell in another half a litre of water and sieve again to obtain the prawn stock. (If a food processor is not available, boil the prawn heads and shells in one litre of water and simmer for about 20 minutes.)

Combine the prawn stock with the bone stock and add a third of the fried shallots, 3 tbsp sugar and 1 tsp salt. Include the lean meat and bring to the boil. Simmer for about half an hour.

Just before serving, bring the soup to a boil and add the peeled prawns. Remove the prawns from the soup when they are no longer transparent and use as a garnish. Remove the lean meat and slice thinly for use as a garnish.

Serve buffet style or individually in bowls. The beansprouts go in first, kangkong and then the mee and/or bee hoon. Next, pour in the soup with a few ribs. Garnish with sliced pork, prawns, fried sliced shallots, bak eu phok and chilli oil paste.

MALAY INFLUENCE

THIS CHAPTER IS ABOUT PENANG FOOD with predominantly Malay influence. The dishes featured here have been cooked in my Penang Nonya family for years and are, in many respects, not much different from the Malay versions.

Malay curries are referred to as *gulai* in the Northern states of Malaysia, and the Nonyas in Penang widely use the word to describe curry dishes. However, the term is not included in the name of many classic spicy Malay dishes like Assam Pedas (sour hot curry), Beef Rendang (dry beef curry) and Sambal Udang (spicy prawns).

The main Malay dishes are characterized by the use of creamy coconut milk (santan), sour tamarind (some varieties are also sweet), hot chillies, shallots, garlic, lemongrass (serai) and fragrant root gingers like turmeric (kunyit), galanagal (lengkuas) and cekur. Many leaves and shoots like limau purut (kaffir lime leaf), cekur leaves, daun kadok (a variety of wild pepper leaf) and kesom (*Polygonum* or chien hong in Penang Hokkien), are also used together with a key Southeast Asian ingredient – belacan (dried shrimp paste).

Malay cooking has also been influenced by the use of seed spices like coriander, fennel and cumin brought over by Indian and Arab traders in the 14th century. Gulai Ayam or Gulai Kay to the Penang Nonyas, is a chicken curry that uses such spices.

Malay dishes, like curries, are simpler than the Nonya equivalents. Different varieties of *gulai* are flavoured with different herbs and, in general, one or at most two herbs are used in a dish. For example, kesom is used for Assam Pedas and Indian curry leaves are used for fish curry, unlike more recent fusion curries which mix several herbs together

Traditionally, the ingredients are pounded in a *batu lesong* – a granite mortar and pestle (see page 39). The end product of pounding and mixing the wet and the dry ingredients is the *rempah* (spice paste). In Malay cooking, the ingredients are not so finely pounded. If the spices are to be more finely ground, what is used is the *batu giling* – a granite slab and roller originating from India. Today, food processors can be used, but buying a processor with the appropriate blade that chops finely is critical. Not all electric food processors can grind wet ingredients finer than the *batu giling*.

In the days before mechanical rollers, whole dried cuttle-fish were pounded with a hammer. This Malay hawker was a fixture at the Chinese Swimming Club. His father sold Malay Laksa.

Normally, the *rempah* is gently fried (*tumis* in Malay) with coconut oil in an earthen pot (*belanga*) until it is fragrant, after which fish, prawns, chicken or other permissible meat is added. The Malays traditionally lived close to the coast, hence seafood provided the main source of protein. In recent times, beef, mutton and lamb are served more often.

A *senduk* (ladle made from coconut shell, see top of page 35) is used for stirring and scooping up the dish. Today the Chinese wok, known as *kuali* in Malay is commonly used for cooking Malay dishes.

Rice was extensively grown in Penang Island when I was young. Coconut trees grew around the padi fields and in the kampongs. If you cook rice with coconut milk, you have a very tasty Nasi Lemak. In fact, you could eat Nasi Lemak with just Sambal Belacan and sliced cucumber although you could complement it with other dishes like fried sambal fish.

Sambal is an important condiment which accompanies every meal. The basic one is Sambal Belacan, which has been adopted by the Penang Nonyas and the Penang Hainanese. Chillies and toasted belacan are pounded in the *lesong* (mortar) until fine and served with a squeeze of calamansi lime (limau kesturi in Malay or keat lah in Penang Hokkien). The Hainanese version is more liquid; they use vinegar instead of lime.

Nasi Ulam is a Malay dish with Thai influence. *Ulam* is a Malay generic term for a mixture of roots, fruits and a variety of edible leaves, including *puchok* – the young shoots before they turn green. The edible ones are from trees such as mango, cashew nut and buah petai. Buah petai has a seed with a strong smell which is also eaten raw in *ulam*.

Cakes or desserts (*kuih* in Malay) do not form part of the daily Malay meals but are partaken in between as snacks and served on festive occasions like weddings and birthdays. Grated coconut and coconut milk (santan) are two important ingredients in Malay and Nonya desserts. The grated fresh coconut kernel is used in sweets and desserts like Kuih Kosui and Ondeh-Ondeh. Inti, grated coconut cooked with brown sugar, is an important part of many desserts like Pulut Inti (blue steam glutinous rice) and Kuih Koci. Santan is as an ingredient in most *kuih*; it is also used as a topping in sago pudding and black glutinous rice (Pulut Hitam in Malay or Bee Ko Moi in Penang Hokkien).

Coconut Oil

Traditionally, coconut oil is used for Malay cooking. In the old days we were able to buy commercially processed coconut oil from our neighbourhood Chinese sundry shop (*chai tiam ma* in Hokkien) where we bought virtually all our provisions. We also prepared our own virgin coconut oil which was more fragrant than the commercial product. My mother squeezed santan from the grated coconut and left it to stand in a *kuali* until the oil separated. Low heat was then applied to evaporate the water. What remained was the fragrant virgin coconut oil and some crust. This crust is used in some Mee Siam recipes. My mother would sometimes grate the older coconuts which are not so suitable for cooking. These are the coconuts which have just germinated, when the embryo called haustorium (*tamong* in Malay) starts growing within the coconut and the kernel is not so firm. The small or medium size *tamong* is sweet and tasty. The large ones are tasteless.

Recent studies suggest that homemade coconut oil preserve some of the original ingredients of the coconut which are destroyed when copra – from the dried kernel of the coconut – is commercially processed to extract the oil. These studies suggest the high lauric acid content of virgin coconut oil builds up the body's immunity much like mother's milk. Lauric acid is destroyed in the commercial processing of refined coconut oil because of high heat or chemical processing.

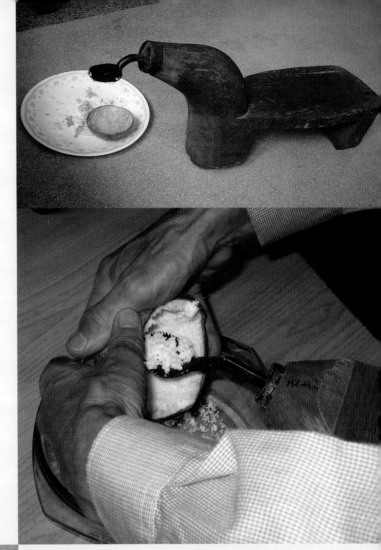

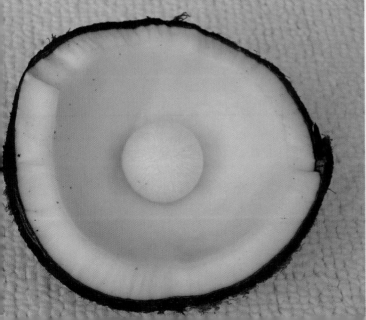

A greeting card, circa 1950s, showing padi being harvested.

A saddle, fashioned from a solid piece of wood with a metal scraper attached, was used for grating coconut. One sat on the seat, weighing the implement down as one scraped the coconut on the serrated blade.

A tambong, the embryo of a germinating coconut. The small ones are sweet and tasty!

UBIQUITOUS PRODUCTS
FROM THE COCONUT PALM

The coconut tree (*Cocos nucifera*) is 'the tree with a thousand uses'. It not only provides ingredients for food, but is also used to make utensils and accessories for cooking. Its trunk is used as timber and its leaves for thatching, weaving and as fuel. The husk of the coconut can also be used as fuel, and processed as coir fibre for ropes, mattresses and rooting medium.

Young coconut provides us with nutritious coconut water and the smooth, jelly-like flesh. The white flesh of the mature coconut is used extensively in Malay and Nonya

No. 126.   MALAY HUTS, TANJONG TOKONG, PENANG.

cooking. This kernel, when dried, is also used as animal feed. Coconut oil is used for food in pastry, margarine and condiments. It is used commercially for making soap, cosmetics, hair and body oil and also oil for lamps.

These days, we no longer have to husk, crack or grate coconuts because we can buy coconuts ready grated. Thus, the present generation does not know how to crack a coconut, much less husk one. A husked

coconut has what looks like two eyes and a mouth. Hold the coconut with these features facing sideways. Use the back of a chopper to hit the coconut hard along its middle. A second or third blow would be needed to fully crack the nut. A small metal spatula is used to separate the kernel from the shell.

Grated coconut flesh and coconut milk (santan) are two important ingredients in Malay and Nonya cooking. Coconut is traditionally grated using a serrated metal grater mounted on a small wooden saddle. One sits astride with the grater in front. Holding half a coconut, one scrapes the kernel against the grater. Today, some graters are designed to fold up and pack flat.

Grated coconut from the scraper is considered too coarse for desserts by elderly Nonyas. Instead, they use a *parut*, a wooden block with short thin brass wires.

Gated coconut is put in a muslin bag and squeezed to obtain *pati santan* or *santan thau* (head) – concentrated coconut milk. Salt is traditionally added to the santan so that it will not go sour. More santan can be recovered from the grated coconut by adding hot water and squeezing a second and, sometimes, a third time to yield thin coconut milk. The Nonyas refer to this as *santan boey* (tail).

The sap collected from incising the flower clusters of the coconut tree can be made into several edible products: Palm sugar (Gula Melaka), toddy, arrack, vinegar, and yeast. To make Gula Melaka, the fresh sap is boiled to reduce the water content and obtain a syrup

which is traditionally poured into bamboo sections to solidify into cylinders.

If left to ferment slightly, the sap would become toddy, a sour brew – a poor man's alcoholic drink. The unpleasant smelling toddy used to be sold at government-controlled shops all over the then Malaya and Singapore. It was used in many old recipes in place of yeast as a rising agent. I recall buying toddy for my mother at the toddy store at Pulau Tikus. In the process, I had to steer clear of the customers who had had too much to drink. Further fermentation of toddy gives rise to vinegar while arrack is the alcoholic spirit obtained from the distillation of toddy.

The other edible part of the coconut tree is the bud or *umbut* in Malay. This is the portion just above the trunk where the shoots emerge. As it is only available if the tree has been felled, it is a rare delicacy – sweet, crunchy and fragrant. The other edible part is the embryo or haustorium of a newly germinating coconut; *tamong* in Malay.

Coconut trees have leaflets on either side of the leaf stalk. The different parts of the leaves are used in the preparation of Malay and Nonya foods like satay, ketupat and otak. The young, yellowish green leaflets are used for wrapping rice in ketupat and for weaving. In the other Malaysian states and Singapore, the mature leaflets are used for wrapping Panggang Otak (spicy fish cake); the Penang Nonya otak is steamed in banana leaves, but uses a *lidi* to pin the leaves together.

Lidi (pronounced 'lili' by the Penang Hokkiens) is the midrib of the coconut leaflet obtained by stripping away the leafy parts. The midribs were traditionally used as satay sticks. These midribs, when bunched together, are still used today as brooms, especially in gardens and wet areas.

The *lidi* can be woven into baskets, fruit trays and pot holders known as *lekar* in Malay and *bok keng loak* – literally 'earthen pot down' in Hokkien. The earthen pot or *belanga* used for cooking curry has a round base so the *lekar* is used to hold the pot upright. Both the *belanga* and *lekar* are still used in my mother and auntie's kitchens. Coconut shells are used to make utensils like *senduk* (ladle) for stirring and scooping food. They are also made into various ornaments like money boxes, rings and carvings. The coconut shell can also be used to produce charcoal.

The trunk of the coconut tree was traditionally used to build small bridges and is now made into furniture, chopsticks and home décor accessories. Paper pulp can also be made from the coconut trunk.

NASI LEMAK

Nasi Lemak is a Malay dish that originated in kampongs where coconuts were plentiful. Rice or nasi is the staple food for the Malays; cook the nasi with coconut milk (santan) and we have Nasi Lemak. *Lemak* is the Malay word that describes the creaminess of food, due to the fat in the coconut milk. *Pandanus* leaves are added to give the rice its distinctive fragrance. Nasi Lemak would not be the same without Sambal Belacan. Other traditional accompaniments are fried Ikan Bilis (Whitebait), fried Ikan Kuning (Yellow-striped Scad) and Sambal Kangkong (water convolvulous). In Penang, the Nonyas adopted the dish and served it with fried peanuts, Assam Heh Chien (fried tamarind prawns, see page 44) and sliced cucumber. In addition, our family serves Nasi Lemak with a version of Ikan Assam Pedas with a thicker gravy and slices of fried fish marinated in tamarind or turmeric.

Nasi Lemak is readily available, cooked by the various races in Penang and the rest of Malaysia and Singapore. However, most of the Nasi Lemak that I have tasted recently doesn't quite taste right. It is most probably because too little coconut milk is used in the cooking and the rice is therefore not *lemak* (rich) enough. This recipe makes the nasi really *lemak*!

Traditionally, Nasi Lemak is wrapped in banana leaves. Unfortunately, banana leaves are being replaced by the less environmentally friendly grease-proof brown paper. Modestly priced Nasi Lemak comes with Sambal Belacan and the less expensive garnishes such as Ikan Bilis, fried peanuts and a boiled egg. An up-market version available at the stall on Cantonment Road, next to the Pulau Tikus market, is served with tamarind fried prawn, fried Ikan Kuning, sliced cucumber and, most importantly, good Sambal Belacan. Some stalls or restaurants have upped the ante by serving Nasi Lemak with a variety of curries.

In my youth, we were told to estimate the amount of water needed to cook rice by putting our index finger onto the rice and adding sufficient water till the water level reached the first finger joint. This is a good rule of thumb or should I say, a good rule of index finger! The method has always worked. We also vary the amount of water a little to account for the age of the rice. Newer or newly harvested rice needs less water while older rice needs more water. This rule is a good guide for cooking Nasi Lemak as well, but it is better to use a little less water on account of the additional coconut milk added to the partially cooked rice. This will ensure that the rice grains of the Nasi Lemak do not stick together, is fluffy and not soggy. In short, patience is required, especially if we are cooking larger quantities of Nasi Lemak, because it takes longer to cook than ordinary rice.

You can use freshly squeezed coconut milk or commercially concentrated coconut milk in UHT packs. However, do try different brands available to you to find one that is the closest to fresh coconut milk.

Nasi Lemak is a dish that's easy to serve at picnics. Here, my grandmother, aunt, uncle and mother are enjoying a continous buffet on the beach at Telok Bahang.

Nasi Lemak
(Serves 6)

450 g long grain rice
1 coconut, grated or 400 g grated coconut or
    220 ml concentrated coconut milk
400 ml water
2 tsp salt or to taste
3 *Pandanus* leaves
3 cm old ginger, skinned and smashed

Wash the rice and repeat until the water is clear.

Slit each *Pandanus* leaf lengthwise into two, fold into two and tie each leaf into a knot.

If using grated coconut
Squeeze the grated coconut through muslin or a cloth with a coarse weave to get as much as possible of the first squeeze coconut milk (*santan thau)*. Set aside. Add the salt to the santan. Add 200 ml of water to the grated coconut and squeeze again to get a second squeeze or the *santan boey*. Repeat the process with the remaining 200 ml of the water to obtain more of the *santan boey*.

If using commercial Concentrated Coconut Milk
Dilute about 40 ml of the concentrated coconut milk with the water and treat this as the second squeeze or *santan boey*. Use the rest of the concentrated coconut milk as the first squeeze or *santan thau*. Add salt to the santan.

Cooking Nasi Lemak in a rice cooker
Cook the rice with the *santan boey* and the ginger in a rice cooker of 2-litre capacity. After about 10 - 12 minutes, when the rice is boiling, stir with a flat ladle to ensure that the rice does not stick to the bottom of the pot. Repeat after another 10 minutes or when the rice cooker has switched off automatically. Spread the thick coconut milk evenly over the rice. Stir well to mix and put the *Pandanus* leaves on top of the rice. Leave the rice to simmer for at least 30 minutes at the 'keep warm' mode so that the rice absorbs the coconut milk.

The stirring ensures that the rice cooker does not switch off prematurely. Adding coconut milk to the rice over-rides the normal operations of the rice cooker. Normally, the rice cooker automatically turns off when the rice reaches a certain temperature when the rice is cooked. It is not possible to turn on the rice cooker again until the rice at the bottom of the rice pot cools down. The stirring ensures that the bottom of the rice pot remains wet. The temperature will increase if the bottom is dry.

Cooking Nasi Lemak in a saucepan
To cook Nasi Lemak in a saucepan, boil the rice with the second squeeze coconut milk. Turn the heat down to low-simmer once the rice has boiled. Stir the rice after about 10 minutes.

After about another 20 minutes, just before the water in the saucepan dries up, stir the rice again, ensuring that the rice does not stick to the bottom of the pot. Put the *Pandanus* leaves on the rice.

Mix the remaining coconut milk, spread it over the rice and stir well. Leave the rice to simmer on a very low heat for at least 30 minutes so that the coconut milk is absorbed. Invariably, a rice crust called *pnooi phee* in Hokkien will form at the bottom of the pot.

Fluff up before serving with Sambal Belacan, fried Ikan Bilis, fried groundnuts, and sliced cucumber. Other dishes that go with Nasi Lemak are hard-boiled egg, omelete, Ikan Assam Pedas, Sambal Ikan Bilis/Kacang, Sambal Kangkong, fried *assam* prawns, fried Ikan Kuning, and fried sliced fish marinated in tamarind.

Sambal Belacan
(Makes 6 tablespoons)

The Penang Nonya Sambal Belacan is basic, consisting of chillies, belacan and keat lah (calamansi or limau kesturi in Malay). It is not cooked or fried, unlike the sambals in Malacca and Singapore where shallots and/or daun limau perut (kaffir lime leaves) is also added.

Sambal Belacan is served as a condiment, particularly with Malay and Nonya dishes such as Nasi Lemak, birthday noodles and fried mee or bee hoon. There is also the Hainanese version in Penang which is more liquid.

Sambal Belacan is a key ingredient in Nasi Ulam and Kerabu (see pages 45 and 184). It keeps quite well in the freezer so it is convenient to prepare it in bulk.

10 fresh red chillies, stalks removed
25 g (1 tbsp) belacan
6 keat lah or limau kesturi (calamansi limes)

Slice the belacan thinly or fashion it into a thin wafer and grill or toast under low heat till dry and fragrant. You can break up the belacan into pieces during the grilling process.

Remove the seeds from the chillies if you wish and slice the chillies to make it easier to pound. If the sambal is well pounded you won't be able to see the seeds.

Pound the cut chillies till fine, then add the grilled belacan and continue pounding to break up the belacan and to mix it together with the chillies.

Squeeze the juice from the keat lah and mix with the sambal just before serving.

When we pound sambal belacan at home, we usually sit on a low, small stool called a bung ku.

Sambal Ikan Bilis and Kacang

(Serves 6 with other dishes)

Fried Ikan Bilis (Whitebait) and fried kacang (groundnuts) on their own go well with Nasi Lemak. Combining the two in a sambal results in a spicy accompaniment that is even better. This is a basic dry version; some recipes use limau perut (kaffir lime leaves), lemongrass and lime or tamarind juice to give it tang. The main thing is that the Ikan Bilis and the fried groundnuts must stay crispy. There are other versions where the Ikan Bilis is cooked in a sambal sauce.

Ikan Bilis is dried, salted Whitebait or Anchovy that comes in different grades. The ones with less salt, which are more white than grey, cost more. Dried Ikan Bilis is sold whole, head and all, or split into two, with the heads and innards removed. The latter is much healthier because there is less cholesterol. Like salt fish, Ikan Bilis used to be an inexpensive poor man's food. These days, we don't get much Ikan Bilis with our Nasi Lemak if we buy them from the hawker stalls. The beauty of doing our own cooking is that we can have as much Ikan Bilis as we like!

100 g Ikan Bilis (Whitebait or Anchovy),
   rinsed and dried
150 g small groundnuts with skin
8 dried chillies
4 (about 50 g) fresh red chillies
2 cloves garlic
100 g shallots
40 ml water
5 tbsp oil
1 tsp sugar
½ tsp salt

Remove the stalks and seeds from the dried chillies and soak the chillies for about 10 minutes. Likewise, remove the stalks and seeds from the fresh red chillies and slice the chillies into smaller pieces for easier grinding. Peel the shallots, discarding the root ends, and slice coarsely. Peel and smash the garlic. Grind all the rempah ingredients together in a liquidizer, adding about 40 ml of water to ensure that the rempah is properly ground.

Heat 5 tbsp of the oil in a wok. When the oil is hot and nearly smoking, fry the groundnuts over medium heat for about 10 minutes till just before the skins of the groundnuts turn brown. Remove the nuts from the oil, and drain on kitchen paper to remove excess oil.

Fry the Ikan Bilis in the same oil for about 10 minutes till the fish turns light brown. Remove from the oil and drain on kitchen paper.

Remove all but one tablespoon of oil from the wok. Fry the rempah till fragrant. This will take about 10 minutes. Add about 20 ml of water and mix into a thinner paste and fry for about 2 minutes. Add sugar and salt, the fried groundnuts and Ikan Bilis, mix thoroughly with the rempah and serve.

The fried groundnuts and the fried Ikan Bilis can also be served separately without the sambal.

Ikan Goreng

This is about frying fish the Malay way. Ikan Kuning (Yellow-striped Scad) is fried with kunyit (turmeric). It was commonly served with Nasi Lemak by hawkers because it used to be a cheap fish. Ikan Kuning is a small fish about 12 cm in length. All parts can be eaten, except the vertebra, if it is well fried. Hence, there is no need to trim the fins although Nonyas always do so! Fortunately, these fish do not have scales to remove.

To prevent the fish from sticking to the frying pan, make sure that the pan is clean and well heated up before oil is added. Dry the fish, and put it in only when the oil is hot. It is best to turn the fish only once. My cousin sprinkles a bit of flour on both sides of the fish to prevent it from sticking.

Selar or Yellowtail can also be fried whole in the same way. Bawal Hitam or Black Pomfret is normally sliced, marinated in tamarind paste and shallow fried. It can also be fried whole, in which case two or three slits are cut on each side of the fish.

10 Ikan Kuning (Yellow-striped Scad)
1 tsp ground kunyit (turmeric)
½ tsp salt
Flour

Remove the gills and gut the fish. Mix the salt with the ground turmeric and spread the mixture with your hands evenly onto the fishes. Add a little water to the mix, if necessary. Lightly sprinkle flour on both sides of each fish.

Heat up the pan and, when it is hot, add the oil. Fry the fish in two lots, turning them once when the side being cooked turns golden brown. Remove from the oil and drain. Serve with Nasi Lemak or rice.

The problem with small fish like Ikan Kuning is that a lot of effort is needed to remove the gills and to gut them. Still, the old generation Nonyas would also cut off the fins and trim the tail.

This dry version of Ikan Assam Pedas goes well with Nasi Lemak. The usual, wet version is eaten with plain rice.

IKAN ASSAM PEDAS
(Serves 6 with other dishes)

The Malay name describes this curry – it is sour or *assam* and spicy hot or *pedas*; *ikan* is 'fish' in Malay. Ikan Assam Pedas is a simple Malay fish curry using some common ingredients employed in Malay cooking – belacan (prawn paste), tamarind, serai (lemongrass), chillies, shallots, garlic and kunyit (turmeric). It is the lemongrass and the addition of kesom that gives Ikan Assam Pedas its distinctive flavour. Kesom (*Polygonum*), a minty herb commonly used in Southeast Asia, is an important ingredient in various laksas from Malaysia and Singapore. Some recipes use assam gelugor to give the Ikan Assam Pedas a more sour taste. Assam gelugor should not be confused with assam, which is tamarind. Called assam phoi in Penang Hokkien, assam gelugor is commonly used in Malay/Nonya dishes. It is a fruit which looks like a large persimmon and is yellow when ripe. My aunt and uncle had a tree in their garden when they lived in Cantonment Road. Some tamarinds are more sour than others, so it is better not to use all the tamarind juice when boiling the *rempah*. The remaining tamarind juice can be added later if the dish is not sour enough. Some recipes also add pineapple which makes the Ikan Assam Pedas a bit too sweet for my taste.

In our family, a version of this curry with thicker gravy is served with Nasi Lemak. We prefer a drier version because we do not want the curry to overwhelm the taste of the coconut rice.

Ikan Assam Pedas is a healthy dish because no oil is used. The *rempah* is traditionally boiled, not fried in oil (*tumis*) as is done for some other curries, However, there is a variation in which the *rempah* is fried without any oil.

Nowadays, there are many other variations and deviations of Ikan Assam Pedas, some of which I personally consider as contemporary fusion dishes. It is now not uncommon to see ladies' finger and tomatoes added. These are two ingredients which I associate with the Southern Indian fish curry (see page 145). I also often find torch ginger buds (bunga kantan) in Ikan Assam Pedas. If you prefer the bunga kantan flavour in a traditional fish curry, you might as well go for Gulai Tumis (page 135) – another Nonya/Hainanese fish curry!

500 gm fish (Mackerel or Pomfret)
1 tbsp tamarind
1 tsp belacan
6 dried chillies
5 fresh red chillies
100 g shallots
1 cm x 2.5 cm diameter fresh kunyit (turmeric)
3 stalks serai (lemongrass)
4 large sprigs (about 25 g) kesom (*Polygonum*)
1 tsp salt
1 tbsp sugar
800 ml water

If Ikan Assam Pedas is to be served with Nasi Lemak, the amount of water used in this recipe should be reduced by about 300 ml.

Soak the tamarind in the 50 ml of water for about 15 minutes. Squeeze the tamarind with your fingers through a sieve to separate the pulp from the fibre. Reserve the thick tamarind juice.

Either slice the belacan thinly or fashion it into a thin wafer; grill or toast till dry and slightly dark brown. Alternatively, use 3 tsp of powdered belacan.

Remove the stalks and the seeds from the dried chillies and soak the chillies in water for about 15 minutes. Wash the fresh chillies, remove the seeds and the white ribs if you prefer this *gulai* to be mildly hot; coarsely slice the chillies.

Peel the shallots, cut off and discard the root portions and slice the shallots finely. Remove the skin from the kunyit and chop the kunyit up. Cut off and discard the leafy portion of the lemongrass stalks, keeping only the white portion which is approximately 5 cm from the root. Cut off the roots, smash the stalks and finely slice two of the stalks to make them easier to pound or grind. Reserve the other stalk for later use.

Pound or grind the belacan, dried and fresh chillies, shallots and lemongrass into a fine *rempah* paste with a mortar and pestle or a food processor. It is better to pound the lemongrass and the dried chillies first as they are harder to grind, then the fresh chillies and the shallots.

Clean the fish and cut them into slices of about 1.5 cm thickness. Rub the fish slices with the salt.

Boil the *rempah* in the 800 ml of water with the tamarind juice and the kesom. Simmer for about 15 minute, then add the sliced fish and bring to boil. Season with sugar. Simmer for two minutes. Serve.

A tamarind (assam jawa) pod with pulp and seeds.

ASSAM UDANG GORENG
ASSAM HEH CHIEN
(Serves 6 with other dishes)

Assam Udang Goreng is prawns, with the shells intact, marinated in assam (tamarind) and fried till crispy. It goes very well with rice and sambal, and especially with Nasi Lemak. If you buy the Nasi Lemak at Cantonment Road in Penang, you will get some fried assam prawns and fried fish with sliced cucumber.

The prawns can be eaten, shell and all, if the prawns are not too big. The white-shelled prawns have thinner shells than the darker grey prawns. If you use larger prawns, you will have to peel the shells before you eat them.

Many in our Ong families are not prawn eaters; it is probably all in the genes. We are more like social prawn eaters, taking the occasional prawn and letting others who better appreciate prawns have more. However, when the prawns are fried till crispy like in Assam Heh Chien and Heh Chnee (prawn fritters, see page 95), we appreciate them very much!

250 g medium-sized prawns
30 g (1½ tbsp) assam (tamarind), seeds removed
1 small cucumber
½ tsp salt
½ tsp sugar
1 tsp dark soya sauce
50 ml water
Oil

Soak the tamarind in 50 ml of hot water for about 20 minutes. Squeeze the tamarind with your fingers through a sieve to separate the pulp from the fibre which is to be discarded. Mix the thick tamarind juice with the salt, sugar and the dark soya sauce to make the marinade.

Remove the legs of the prawns. Cut off the feelers and the sharp saw-like tips on the heads using kitchen scissors. Wash the prawns, dry and thoroughly mix with the marinade. Keep in the refrigerator for at least an hour.

Heat up the oil in a hot wok and add the prawns, a few at a time, with some marinade, and fry on low or medium heat for about 8 to 10 minutes till the prawns are crispy but before the tamarind in the marinade turns black. The fried marinade gives a lovely aromatic flavour. The low heat ensures that the oil will not splash. Remove and drain on kitchen paper. Serve with sliced cucumber and Sambal Belacan.

KACANG GORENG SAMBAL
FRIED SAMBAL LONG BEANS
(Serves 6 with other dishes)

This is a Nonya dish with Malay origins, using fresh ingredients like garlic, chillies, shallots and belacan for the *rempah*. Some santan (coconut milk) is added to make it more *lemak* (creamy, in Malay). The vegetable is yard long beans – kacang panjang in Malay or chai tau in Penang Hokkien dialect. The long beans are fried with prawns and the *rempah*. The Malay version uses dried shrimp but my mother's recipe uses fresh prawns as well. This dish goes well with rice.

This was one of the first dishes that I cooked all by myself. It was part of the test to gain the cookery badge when I was a young Boy Scout. I also had to cook rice and toffee apple! (The toffee apple recipe came from our Boy Scout manual from England.)

As a child, I was told that the long beans should not be cut but should be broken into lengths of about 3 to 4 cm, after the stalk and the tip were removed. This is quite easily done as the young beans are brittle.

This is a traditional Malay dish; the chillies and the shallots should be coarse, hence the *rempah* should not be pounded till fine. It is therefore preferable to use the *lesong* instead of a food processor.

300 g long beans
100 g fresh prawns
20 g dried shrimp
6 (about 50 g) shallots
2 cloves garlic
4 (about 50 g) fresh chillies
1 tsp belacan
2 tbsp coconut milk or cow's milk
2 tbsp oil
250 ml water
Pinch of salt

Soak the dried prawns in water for about ½ hour. Grill the sliced belacan till crispy but not burnt.

Smash the garlic with the side of the chopper and remove the skin. Peel the shallots and cut off the root ends. Wash, de-seed and cut the chillies into pieces. If you like the dish spicy hot leave the seeds in.

Pound the garlic first, then the cut chillies, shallots, dried prawns and the grilled belacan in a mortar (*lesong*) or grind coarsely in a food processor.

Wash the long beans. Break off and discard the stalk and also the tip of each bean. Break each bean into lengths of about 3 cm.

Wash and shell the prawns. Devein and marinate with a pinch of salt.

Heat the wok and when it is hot, put in the oil. Stir-fry the *rempah* for about 10 minutes until it is fragrant. Add about 20 ml water if the *rempah* sticks to the pan.

Put in the prawns. When they are half cooked, add the long beans and the 250 ml of water. Fry for another 10 minutes till the long beans becomes dark green and soft. Finally, stir in the 2 tablespoons of coconut milk.

NASI ULAM
HERBAL SALAD RICE

Ulam is a collective term for an assortment of edible plant shoots, leaves, flowers and roots which are normally finely sliced and eaten raw. Young edible leaves, called *pucuk* in Malay, come from the mango, cashew-nut and petai trees. *Ulam* is the Malay equivalent of a green salad. It is often served with Sambal Belacan.

Nasi Ulam is Malay rice salad with Thai influence which has been adopted by the Nonyas of Penang. It is a balanced meal by itself, with rice mixed with salt fish, flaked fish or prawns, Kerisek (fried grated coconut) and the *ulam* from plants that grow in the garden or in the kampongs.

Some of the familiar *ulam* used in Penang are the rhizomes from varieties of gingers such as common ginger, kunyit (turmeric) and lengkuas (galangal), leaves from some gingers like cekur and bunga kantan, the flower bud of the torch ginger (see page 181). Other ulams are daun kesom (*Polygomun*) which is used in fish curries and Assam Laksa, daun limau purut (kaffir lime leaf) which is used in Lemak Laksa and lemak curries and otak, and daun kaduk from the pepper family which is commonly used in Penang and Thai food. Serai (lemongrass) is an important ingredient for Nasi Ulam because of its lemony flavour. Only the white stem near the root is used.

One not so familiar *ulam* ingredient, especially to the younger generation is daun kentut (*Paederia scandens*) known as pang phooi hueh in Penang Hokkien. The leaves, when crumpled, smells of the gas that is expelled when we break wind and *kentut* is the Malay word for it. It is a creeper that produces clusters of little bell-shaped flowers.

Penang Nasi Ulam is different from Nasi Kerabu that comes from other Malaysian states, like Kelantan, that borders Thailand. The vegetables used in Nasi Kerabu include beansprouts, long beans and cucumber – not commonly used in Penang. This Thai influence did not extend to Penang. The rice is coloured blue using colouring obtained from the bunga telang (blue pea flower). This colouring is not common in Penang Nasi Ulam although it is used to colour the glutinous rice in Pulut Inti, a common Penang Nonya/Malay dessert. Noni leaf shoots (daun kudu or *Morinda citrifolia*) are also used in the Kelantanese version of Nasi Ulam.

This recipe is based on one from my wife's family.

The *ulam* should be very finely sliced. The way to do it is to roll the bigger leaves together into a very tight cylinder and slice finely with a sharp knife. For the smaller leaves, stack them up and slice as thinly as possible. There is a lot of cutting to do for Nasi Ulam.

It is more convenient to prepare the Kerisik and the Sambal Belacan in bulk. Pack them in small packages and keep them in the freezer for future use.

Daun kentut (*Paederia scandens*)

Nasi Ulam
(Serves 12)

900 g rice
300 g dried shrimp
300 g salt fish
600 g Red Snapper, seared*
2 tbsp oil
Salt to taste

Ulam to be Finely Sliced or Chopped:
100 g young ginger
5 cm x 1.5 cm diameter piece kunyit (turmeric)
8 cm x 3 cm diameter piece lengkuas (galangal)

3 bunga kantan (torch ginger buds)

20 daun limau purut (kaffir lime leaves)
3 sprigs duan kesom (*Polygonum*)
20 leaves daun kentut (*Paederia scandens*)

50 leaves daun kadok (*Piper sarmentosum*)
2 leaves daun cekur (*Kaempferia galangal*)
2 daun kunyit (turmeric leaves)

3 stalks serai (lemongrass)

120 g shallots
2 cloves garlic

½ coconut (skinned and grated for Kerisik)

10 fresh chillies (approx. 120g)
1 tbsp belacan

* Alternatively, 500 g small prawns can be used.

Wash and the drain the rice and cook with about 1 litre of water. The rice should be dry and grainy for Nasi Ulam. Leave the rice to stand for at least an hour after it is cooked to allow it to absorb excess water.

Wash the dried prawns and soak in water for about 10 minutes, then pound in a mortar (*lesong*) or grind in a food processor.

Cut the salt fish into slices of about ½ cm thickness and shallow fry in oil till crispy. Break the pieces into bits by hand. Alternatively, grill the pieces in an oven or ovenette and then break into small bits.

Fry the fish in 2 tbsps of oil. Remove the skin and flake the fish finely.

If fresh prawns are used, wash the prawns, remove the heads and devein. Sprinkle some salt and steam or boil the prawns till cooked. Remove and cool before removing the shells. Chop up the meat into 3 or 4 mm pieces.

Slicing the *Ulam*
Remove the skin of the roots: young ginger, tumeric (kunyit) and galangal (lengkuas). Slice thinly, cut into thin strips and then cut across the strips into bits as fine as you can.

Cut the bunga kantan into two lengthwise, and slice finely from the tip of the flower, stopping short of the stalk.

For the daun limau purut, duan kesom and daun kentut, stack the each type of leaf one on top of another and slice as thinly as you can.

Roll the daun kadok, cekur leaves and daun kunyit leaves tightly together into a cylinder and slice as finely as possible. You may wish to cut the sliced strips into shorter sections.

Cut off and discard the leafy parts of the lemongrass (serai). Remove the outer layers of the stalk and cut each stalk into two lengthwise, and then slice thinly, starting from the top end of the serai and stopping short of the root end, which is a bit woody.

Peel the shallots and cut off the root end. Cut each bulb longitudinally and slice each half thinly across.

Smash up the garlic and remove the skin. Chop the garlic very finely.

Kerisek
To make Kerisik, fry the grated coconut over a very low fire till golden brown. Remember that the Kerisik will continue to brown after it has been taken off the heat, so do not overcook. Pound finely.

Sambal Belacan
To make Sambal Belacan, slice the belacan thinly or fashion it into a thin wafer and grill or toast under low heat till dry and fragrant. Break up the belacan into pieces during the grilling. Remove the seeds from the chillies and slice them to make it easier to pound. Pound the cut chillies till fine, then add the grilled belacan and continue pounding to break up the belacan and to mix it with the chillies.

Assembly
To assemble the Nasi Ulam, fluff up the rice and make sure that it is not lumpy. Place the rice in a large mixing bowl and add the salt fish, the flaked fish or the steamed or boiled prawns, the Sambal Belacan and the Kerisik. Mix well. Finally add the sliced *ulam* leaves, spreading them and mixing them evenly into the rice. Add salt to taste. Serve.

A selection of ulam herbs on a large kunyit leaf (clockwise from top): daun kadok, daun cekur, daun limau purut, daun kesom, daun kentut and mint leaves.

ROTI JALA
FISHNET CREPE

Lacy pancake is a good description for Roti Jala, a traditional Malay dish which has been adopted by the Nonyas. *Roti* is 'bread' in Malay and *jala* is 'fishing net'. So, Roti Jala could be more elegantly interpreted as fish net crepe. A recipe in *Female Cookbook 1981* refers to this dish as Roti Renda, *renda* being 'lace' in Malay. Therefore, a properly made Roti Jala should look like a fish net or lace, with a lot of gaps between the thin strings. To keep in step with the Internet age, Roti Jala should perhaps be re-branded as Roti.www.

Roti Jala batter is made by mixing flour, egg and coconut milk. It will be yellow if sufficient eggs are used, although a bit of *kunyit* (turmeric) is often added to enhance the colour.

The basic ingredients for Roti Jala batter have not changed. What has changed is the way the batter is poured on a hot frying pan to create the lacy pattern. In my distant past, I have seen Malay and *mamak* hawkers using banana leaves and *lidi* to make a small funnel for drizzling the batter over the pan. The inventive Nonyas most probably went to Chinese tin-smiths and ordered the Roti Jala cup. It is basically a cup made of brass, tin or copper with four to six small funnels soldered to the bottom. There is also a more user-friendly design which has the funnels on the side to allow you to better control the flow of the batter. With advances in plastic mouldings, Roti Jala cups are now more commonly made of plastic.

The Nonyas made everything very finely. Their beads and beadwork are exquisite and, in cooking, they cut and slice ingredients very meticulously and finely. This characteristic extends to making Roti Jala. The lace of the Roti Jala made by the older generation is really very delicate. It looks easy, but to make it well is an art which requires practice and experience. Some pictures of so-called Roti Jala posted on the Internet look more like pancakes with holes in them!

Roti Jala is cooked on one side only, unlike crepes or pancakes which are cooked on both sides. Once cooked, it is folded into a semicircle, then into a quarter and finally into one eighth. They are then arranged eight in a stack on a round serving dish. If they are not folded and just stacked one on top of another it would be difficult to separate a Roti Jala from the one below. This is how we prepare and serve Roti Jala in our family. Some families may fold their Roti Jala into quarters, while others roll them up.

The proper way to eat Roti Jala is to unfold each piece and have it with a generous amount of curry sauce. Hence it is easier to eat with your fingers. In our family we always eat it with Gulai Kay – Nonya chicken curry cooked Malay style (see page 53). It can, of course, be eaten with other curries.

Nowadays, Roti Jala is a popular dish among Muslims for breaking fast during Ramadan (Muslim fasting month) and also for other festive celebrations.

Roti Jala

600 g flour
½ tsp salt
6 eggs
100 ml milk or coconut milk squeezed
   from ½ coconut, grated
850 ml water
Oil
Paper tissue for oiling pan

Roti Jala Batter

Sieve the flour into a mixing bowl and add the salt. Using a food processor, beat the eggs one at a time into the flour mixture. Now add the milk or coconut milk gradually, stirring to obtain a smooth, thick paste. Finally, include water a little at a time and stir well. If too much water is added at once, it will be difficult to get rid of the lumps in the batter. If the batter is still lumpy, sieve it, otherwise the lumps will block the funnels of the Roti Jala cup.

Test the consistency of the batter through the Roti Jala cup. The batter flowing from the funnels should come out in continuous streams. If it comes out in droplets, the batter is too thick. Add more water and repeat the test. If it is too watery, add more flour and mix well to avoid lumps. Let the batter sit for at least 30 minutes before making the Roti Jala.

Making Roti Jala

Heat up a non-stick pan. Use a paper tissue to coat a thin layer of oil all over the pan.

Place the Roti Jala cup over a bowl to collect the batter that flows out through the funnels. Ladle batter into the cup till it is about half to three quarter full. Hold the bowl with one hand and the cup with the other. Put both over the pan, remove the bowl and move the cup, making circular or figure-of-eight patterns to form a lacy crepe of about 20 cm in diameter. The aim is to make a uniform, thin crepe. The thickness of the web is dependent on the speed which the cup is moved over the pan and on the thickness of the batter. Return the cup to the bowl once you have a lacy crepe.

The Roti Jala is ready when it separates from the pan at the edge. Lift the pan and tilt it to allow the Roti Jala to slide onto a plate. Fold the crepe into two, then into a quarter and one eighth. Arrange on a serving plate.

Repeat with remaining batter. After making a few Roti Jala, use paper tissue to oil the pan again. This may also be necessary if bits of the Roti Jala are stuck on the pan. Serve with chicken curry (see page 53). The Roti Jala should be unfolded before eating.

GULAI AYAM
GULAI KAY

Gulai Ayam is a Malay chicken curry cooked by the Nonyas in Penang and called Gulai Kay in Hokkien. My mother cooked this curry regularly at home. The use of dried spices like coriander, cumin, fennel and cinnamon suggests that this dish has strong Indian influence, but curry leaves are not used. Traditionally, coconut oil is used for frying the *rempah*, but since it is not readily available these days, a healthy oil like canola is preferred.

Potato is an integral part of Gulai Kay. It is very popular with my children, nieces and nephews. Gulai Kay is normally eaten with rice, hence the generous amount of curry gravy. It is also served with Roti Jala (see page 51) and Nasi Kunyit (yellow glutinous rice).

The preparation of the *rempah* or spice mix for the *gulai* described here is the traditional method. The dried spices are prepared first before they are mixed with the wet spices. Toasting the dried spice before grinding brings out their flavours.

My cousin, Sandy, still grinds her *rempah* using the *batu giling* which consists of a flat granite slab of about 50 x 30 cm and a cylindrical granite rolling pin of about 40 cm long and 10 cm in diameter. The surface of the granite slab is flat but rough. The granite pin is not rolled up and down the slab, but one slides it instead to grind the spices. *Batu giling* can be found in most Nonya households in Penang, tucked away in the kitchen or backyard of older houses. We still have a set at my mother's house. It has not been used for many years. When I was young, an Indian lady used to come to our house to *giling* the *rempah*. Later, my mother took the spices to another Indian lady down the road for grinding. You can still buy a brand new *batu giling* today in Penang's Little India near Queens Street.

If traditional grinding tools are used, the dried chillies should be soaked in water for about 15 minutes before grinding. The *rempah* can be ground very finely with the *batu giling*. Normally, for Malay *gulai*, the fresh ingredients like chillies and onions are not so finely ground. However, this curry has a strong Indian influence, hence the *rempah* should be ground finely.

A *lesong* can be used for pounding the dry spices but it is not as efficient as the *batu giling*. If you are using an electric grinder, grind the dry spices first, then add the wet ones. This is because a wet grinder cannot grind the seed spices very well.

If preparing curry powder is too troublesome for you, there are many brands of curry powder available in the market today. About 30 g should be used. When we were living in London we used the Alagappa curry powders that we brought from Penang. There were not that many brands of curry powder in those days.

The author (left) and a friend preparing chicken at the Coronation scout camp.

Gulai Ayam
(Serves 10 with other dishes)

1 (approx. 1.2 kg) chicken
500 g potatoes

Curry powder
10 dried chillies
4 tbsp ketumba (coriander)
1 tsp jintan manis (fennel)
1 tsp jintan puteh (cumin)

1 coconut, grated and squeezed for coconut milk
   or 220 ml concentrated coconut milk
5 cm old ginger
3 cm fresh kunyit (turmeric)
15 (approx. 110 g) shallots

3 tbsp oil
4 cm cinnamon stick
3 cloves
3 lobes of a star anise
1 tsp salt

Curry Powder
Remove the seeds from the dried chillies. Fry the dried chillies for about 2 minutes without oil till slightly pungent. Remove from heat and let it cool.

Fry the ketumbar (coriander) in a pan without oil for about 2 minutes or till slightly aromatic. Set aside. Now fry the jintan puteh (cumin) for about 2 minutes till fragrant but not burnt. Set aside. Lastly, fry the jintan manis (fennel) for also about 2 minutes.

Using an electric grinder, grind the fried dried chillies. Remove. Next, grind the ketumbar, then add the jintan puteh and the jintan manis. Finally, put in the ground chillies and grind to make the curry powder.

To prepare the coconut milk, wrap the grated coconut in a muslin cloth and squeeze out one bowl of thick coconut milk without adding water. Add to this the 1 teaspoon of salt. Now mix 350 ml of water to the remaining grated coconut and squeeze out the diluted santan. Repeat with another 350 ml of water for a second portion of diluted santan.

If commercial concentrated coconut milk is used, dilute 20 ml of it in 700 ml of water to make the thin coconut milk.

Peel and slice the ginger and cut into thin strips of less than 1 mm. Peel the kunyit (turmeric) and cut into smaller pieces for easier grinding. Peel the shallots and slice for easier grinding.

Clean the chicken, remove the skin and fat if you want a healthier dish. Cut into serving pieces. Set aside. Peel the potatoes and cut into quarters or into eighths, depending on the size of the potatoes. Set aside.

Put the dried ground spices or curry powder, shallots and kunyit in a blender; add about 20 ml of water to ensure that the ingredients circulate. The *rempah* is ready when the mixture is homogenous.

Heat up the oil and, when hot, add the *rempah*. Continuously stir or *tumis* the *rempah* for about 10 minutes or till fragrant. Then add the chicken pieces and the cinnamon stick, the cloves and 3 lobes of star anise. Stir to coat the chicken pieces with the *rempah*.

Add the thin coconut milk and the potatoes, bring to boil and simmer for 20 minutes.

Bring to a boil again and add a bowl of thick coconut milk when the chicken is nearly cooked.

Serve with plain rice, Roti Jala or Nasi Kunyit.

BUBUR PULUT HITAM
(Serves 8)

Bubur Pulut Hitam is another traditional Malay dessert adopted and adapted by the Nonyas. It is made from black glutinous rice or pulut hitam and served with fresh coconut milk. *Bubur* is 'porridge', *pulut* is 'glutinous rice' and *hitam* is 'black' in Malay. It is also called Bee Ko Moi, literally translated as glutinous rice porridge from Penang Hokkien. Some recipes add white glutinous rice and sago to make the dessert more glutinous but I find that the texture of the black glutinous rice I use is good enough. However, some black glutinous rice may not be so sticky and adding sago may help.

The Penang Nonyas put dried logan into Bubur Pulut Hitam to give it an additional bite. In the old days, dried longan came whole – shell and all – and the dried flesh had to be removed from the seed. The flesh then was rather thin. Today, dried logan flesh is readily available and the flesh is much thicker. The use of unpolished glutinous rice gives this dessert a bit of crunch. The best black glutinous rice is said to come from Thailand. Like many other Malay and Nonya desserts, *Pandanus* leaves are used to give flavour.

This black porridge is served with a generous helping of coconut milk. Traditionally, salt is added to the coconut milk to prevent it from going sour. Even with refrigerators today, salt is still added; it is part of the traditional taste of this dessert as a little salt accentuates the sweetness of the dessert.

Coconut milk has recently gained a bad name because of the concern about its high saturated fat content. However, fresh coconut milk has a very high percentage of lauric acid, which has potent anti-viral and anti-bacterial properties. In that way, the lauric oils in coconut are similar to the fats in mother's milk. Lauric acid is destroyed once the coconut milk is cooked, so eating coconut products that have not been subjected to high temperatures is good for us. Note that in many curries, the first squeeze santan is put in last. Many Malay and Nonya *kuih* (cakes) use freshly grated coconut and uncooked santan. Young coconuts are also a healthy food.

Coconut milk should not be mixed with Bubur Pulut Hitam before serving. It is normally spooned into individual bowls only when served.

30 g dried longan flesh
½ coconut, grated and squeezed
     or 110 ml UHT concentrated coconut milk
1 tsp salt
125 g black glutionous rice
3 *Pandanus* leaves, knotted
50 g sugar

Soak the dried longan flesh in warm water for at least ½ hour. Break each longan into two or three pieces.

Place the grated coconut in a muslin cloth bag and squeeze out as much of the thick coconut milk as you can. Mix the salt with the coconut milk and refrigerate.

Wash the black glutinous rice and boil in 600 ml of water with the *Pandanus* leaves. Let it simmer for about one hour.

Stir in the dried logan and the sugar with another 200 ml of water. Bring to boil and let it simmer for another 5 minutes. Remove the *Pandanus* leaves.

Serve the Bubur Pulut Hitam in individual bowls. Add a few teaspoonfuls of the santan as you serve.

The Penang Nonyas took the traditional simple Malay dessert, added banana, yam and sweet potato, and transformed it into a colourful dish with many flavours and textures.

PENGAT
(Serves 8)

Pengat is a traditional Malay dessert cooked with santan (coconut milk) and gula melaka, the most well-known one being Pengat Pisang (banana). Other fruits used as the main ingredient are nangka (jackfruit), chempedak (another type of nangka with softer flesh) and labu (pumpkin). More recently, I have seen Pengat Durian. Tuberous root vegetables are also used as the main ingredient to create Pengat Keladi (yam), Pengat Ubi Kayu (tapioca – both fresh and fermented) and Pengat Keledek (sweet potato). Green beans and red beans are also used. The Thais have a dessert similar to pengat.

The Penang Nonyas adopted this dessert and used multiple ingredients – banana, yam and sweet potato – and called it Pengat without any suffix. The preferred banana is pisang raja. *Raja* means 'king' in Malay and so pisang raja is the top banana among the many types available in Malaysia. In addition to the yellow-fleshed sweet potatoes, orange- and purple-fleshed ones have been included as they have become available to give the dessert more colour. Note that the colour of the skin does not correspond with the flesh of the sweet potato; the Japanese ones with purple skin are often orange inside.

Bubur Cha Cha, another Penang Nonya dessert, is related to and derived from Pengat. It includes boiled black-eyed beans, sometimes jagong (maize) and colourful bits of boiled starch and sago. However, there is no banana in Bubur Cha Cha. I do not know why but that is what my mother and others of the older generation claim. Recipes in well-known books by Yeap Joo Kim, Susie Hing and Leong Yee Soo do not have banana in Bubur Cha Cha either. Sugar, instead of gula melaka, is used in Bubur Cha Cha. The sauce for Pengat is thicker because of the use of gula melaka. It is unfortunate that some of the younger generation of Penang food bloggers mix up their Pengat with their Bubur Cha Cha.

When my mother cooks Pengat or Bubur Cha Cha, she cuts the sweet potatoes into diamond shapes. Besides being a more interesting shape, I wonder whether it is done to present a larger surface area for steaming or boiling. However, my cousin, Letticia, tells me that the yam should be cut into rectangular blocks. That is one way of separating the yam from the sweet potatoes! It is not easy to cut the sweet potatoes into the right thickness and into exact shapes because fresh sweet potatoes crumble easily and they are, nowadays, smaller.

I understand that Pengat is a festive dessert like Kuih Ee. Pengat is eaten by the Nonyas during *chap goh meh* which is the fifteen day of the Chinese New Year. However, I don't remember eating Pengat for *chap goh meh* in my family probably because my mother used to cook Pengat and Bubur Cha Cha all year round!

300 g sweet potatoes (white, yellow, orange and purple)
250 g yam
3 small bananas
70 g *gula melaka*
1 coconut, grated or
    220 ml commercial concentrated coconut milk
A pinch of salt
3 *Pandanus* leaves, knotted

Put the grated coconut in a muslin bag and squeeze to obtain the thick coconut milk. Add 250 ml of water to the squeezed coconut and mix thoroughly. Squeeze again. Repeat with the another 250 ml of the water. This is the thin coconut milk.

Alternatively, dilute 20 gm commercial thick coconut milk in 500 ml of water to make the thin coconut milk.

Peel the sweet potatoes. Cut into slices of about 1.5 cm, then into strips of 1.5 cm and finally slice the strips diagonally into diamond shapes with sides of about 3 cm. Keep under water to stop them from turning grey.

Peel the yam and dry the tubers otherwise they will be difficult to handle. Cuts into slices of about 1.5 cm, then into strips of 1.5 cm and finally slice the strips diagonally into diamond shapes with sides of about 3 cm. Keep the cut yam aside.

You can steam the sweet potatoes and the yam, but it is more convenient to boil the yam and sweet potatoes separately for about 6 to 7 minutes till just soft. It is best to boil the different coloured potatoes separately as their cooking times are different, otherwise some potatoes will be softer than others. Use one type of sweet potato if you wish to save on cooking time. Drain and discard the water. Keep the cooked tubers aside.

Break up the gula melaka and dissolve it in half the thin santan and gradually bring to a boil. Meanwhile, peel and slice the bananas diagonally, about 1.5 cm thick, and add to the gula melaka and santan mixture. Turn off the heat when the mixture boils. Set aside.

Boil the rest of the thin santan with the salt, the *Pandanus* leaves, sweet potatoes and yam. Simmer for about 2 to 3 minutes. Add boiled bananas with the gula melaka mixture and bring to the boil. Then add the thick santan, stir well and turn off the fire before it boils. Remove the *Pandanus* leaves.

Pengat can be served hot or chilled, but it should not be served with ice because that dilutes the sauce.

HOKKIEN INFLUENCE

HOKKIEN INFLUENCE ON PENANG FOOD is significant since the majority of the Chinese in Penang originated from southern Fujian Province, China.

The long coastline, the rivers and the rugged mountains of Fujian, where only about one tenth of the land is suitable for agriculture, shaped Hokkien cuisine. The numerous islands on the coast, which provide fishing grounds for crabs, oyster, cuttlefish and a large variety of fish, is the reason that fish and other seafood feature in many Hokkien dishes. From its mountainous forests come ingredients like bamboo shoots, mushrooms, fungi, fruits and nuts.

Life in the province was difficult in the 18th century due to the recurrence of famine, banditry and war. Hence, food was never wasted and any surplus was preserved by drying and pickling. This resulted in salted and pickled products becoming the specialities of the region.

The hard life drove a large number of Hokkiens to leave their homeland for better conditions in Nanyang, literally 'southern oceans', the generic Chinese term for Southeast Asia. So, many Hokkiens settled in Thailand, Indonesia and the Straits Settlements of Singapore, Malacca and Penang. These migrants brought their cuisine and cooking techniques with them.

One clear Hokkien influence on Penang food is the common use of cured ingredients like dried ju hu (cuttlefish), kiam chai (pickled vegetable), kiam hu (salt fish) and chai por (salted vegetable). Penang heritage dishes like Ju Hu Char, Kiam Chai Ark, Steamed Pork with Salt Fish and Koay Teow Kark make stars of these humble fare. Fried salt fish is an indispensable garnish for Gulai Tumis.

Fine slicing technique is also stressed in Hokkien cooking, particularly for seafood, to ensure that the flavour of each ingredient is unlocked. Older Penangites will remember how cuttlefish was so carefully and finely scored in a criss-cross pattern. Some Penang Nonyas still practise this skill as a matter of course. I am amazed how finely my luk kim (sixth aunt) cuts the ingredients for her Koay Pai Ti (see page 85).

The Nonya of old ensured that vegetables and dried ju hu (cuttlefish) were finely and evenly sliced. They even took

Steamboat is a typical Hokkien soup-based dish which includes many types of meat and vegetables.

pains to finely slice the shallot and finely chop the garlic which were fried as condiments and garnishes.

Another characteristic of Hokkien food is the pre-dominance of soupy dishes and porridge. Hokkien Mee (see page 27) is a distinctly Penang hawker food which has noodles, sliced pork and prawns served in soup. Koay Teow Thng is another Penang hawker soup dish with flat rice noodle traditionally served with duck's meat, fish balls and ark huet (coagulated duck's blood).

Dr. Jacqueline Newman, a specialist in Chinese food who donated her lifetime collection of Chinese cookbooks to Stony Brook University, made an interesting observation about Hokkien fare: "Fujian people have a reputation for eating meat and fish in the same dish and for serving as many as five soups in a meal". Likewise, a lot of Penang Hokkien dishes are soup-based and there are many dishes, especially soups that have fish, prawn, chicken and pork mixed together. Good examples are Ean Lor (steamboat) and Chap Chai Thng (mixed vegetable soup). The filling of Choon Piah (a spring roll which is different from Fried Poh Piah) has a mixture of pork, crabs and, in some recipes, prawns, among other ingredients. These dishes were localized by the Penang Nonya and later modified by the Hainanese.

Hokkien food has a reputation for being simple and basic, without embellishments. Dishes widely served in Penang, like Fried Tau Kwa (beancurd) and Tau Eu Bak (pork stewed in soya sauce), are examples of this straight-forward approach. To this list you might add Oh Chien (fried oyster) where the small, glorified barnacle form of the shellfish is simply fired in sweet potato flour, Hokkien style.

Besides being frugal, the Hokkien farmer made the most of any livestock that was slaughtered. Even today, practically every part of livestock is eaten, including the blood from the pig, chicken and duck. Coagulated pig blood is an ingredient in Yong Towfu, and Kali Mee (curry noodles). The Penang Koay Teow Thng is served with duck meat, coagulated duck's blood and sometimes gizzard and liver. And, of course, there is pork fat.

Another characteristic of Hokkien cuisine is the use of various dipping sauces employing tau eu (soya sauce), shallots,

BAK EU PHOK & BAK PHOEY

Pork is an important meat in Hokkien cuisine and lard is widely used. Char Koay Teow would not be the same if it is not fried with *bak eu* (lard), and especially so if bak eu phok is missing. Bak eu phok, lard fried to a crisp, is added as a garnish to many Penang hawker dishes like Hokkien Mee, Wanthan Mee and Koay Teow Thng.

We did not have potato crisps in our time but we had bak eu phok. It may have been sinful but it was crunchy and you could not stop eating it. In my youth, most of the cooking at home used lard, except for curries which used coconut oil. My mother always had a large pot of lard at the ready in her kitchen. In those days, pigs were fed on a poor diet and belly pork was therefore very fat. The layer of fat, sold separately by the butchers, was more than 3 cm thick, which meant that we would have more chunks of bak eu phok to eat!

To make bak eu phok, separate the skin from the fat. Use a sharp knife or chopper, cutting horizontally and slightly downward but avoid cutting through the *bak phoey* (skin). Do not throw away the skin!

Cut the fat into 1 cm cubes. Put in a wok over a low fire and add a bit of water at the start. It is important to stir frequently. The cubes will shrink after giving out the lard. The wok should not too hot otherwise the outside of the fat will be crusty, trapping some lard within. Remove from the wok when the bak eu phok turns light brown Sprinkle on a bit of salt. Eat by itself – *chaik chit tho* (eat for enjoyment)! Otherwise, use as garnish.

The *bak phoey* (skin) that was removed from the bak eu can be dried and deep fried. It is like kerupok (prawn crackers). It can eaten by itself or cooked in soup – to serve as a poor man's substitute for hu peow (fish maw).

Penang kitchens of old would have lard and Bak Eu Pok at the ready.

SUAN YONG CHOR

Suan Yong Chor is a slightly sweet and sour garlic flavoured chilli sauce. The main ingredients are garlic, vinegar and red chillies. It is a mandatory sauce for fried snacks and many traditional Penang food. It comes with Poh Piah Chnee (page 82) sold by the Indian *kuih* men who used to ply the streets of Penang. There was a time when steamed crabs were served with Suan Yong Chor next to the Chinese temple at Tanjong Tokong. Likewise, the vegetarian fried mee and bee hoon sold at popular stalls near Rope Walk and Cintra Street would not taste right without Suan Yong Chor.

Suan Yong Chor was probably the most common chilli sauce in the days before the commercially bottled chilli sauces came into the market. In those days the only commercial product was Lingham's chilli sauce which was made in Logan Road in Penang. The thick and sweet Lingham's chilli sauce was relatively expensive. I remember eating hotdogs with Linghams.

Suan Yong Chor is traditionally prepared in bulk at home and stored in bottles. Its own ingredients help preserve the sauce and there is no need for refrigeration.

It is slightly different from the chillie sauce that goes with Hainanese Chicken Rice in that it does not contain ginger.

This Suan Yong Chor recipe is from my cousin, Sandy.

250 g fresh red chillies
50 g garlic
40 large keat lah or limau kesturi (calamansi)
6 tbsp sugar
½ tsp salt
½ cup water

Squeeze the lime. Wash the chillies and remove the stalks. If a milder sauce is preferred remove the seeds and the white ribs that the seeds are attached to. Cut the chillies into smaller portions.

Smash up the garlic with the side of a chopper, cut off the root ends and peel off the skin. Chop up the garlic coarsely.

Pound the chillies and garlic in a mortar or grind in a food processor. Finally, add the lime juice, salt and sugar

When preparing large quantities of Suan Yong Chor, vinegar can be used in place of lime for convenience. Substitute 3 tablespoons of vinegar for the juice of 40 limes. The ground products are boiled with the vinegar and simmered for 5 minutes before adding the salt and sugar.

garlic, vinegar, sliced chillies and spring onions. Tau eu is an ubiquitous sauce in Hokkien cuisine, and Fujian Province is well known for producing the finest soya sauce. The more mature Penangites are all familiar with the products of Amoy Canning that set up the first soya sauce and canning factory in Amoy, now Xiamen, in Fujian. We commonly refer to soya sauce as tau eu when there are two varieties - dark soya sauce and the light soya sauce or cheow cheng. Light soya sauce is used in place of salt or with salt for cooking most dishes in Penang. It is also commonly added as a condiment to fried fish, meat and soups. Many of my uncles insisted on having a side plate of cheow cheng served with every meal. Some of my cousins still do so today. In Kuala Lumpur, dark soya sauce is more commonly used than light soya sauce. For example, Hokkien Char in KL – known as Hokkien Mee in the rest of Malaysia and Singapore – is dark in colour, unlike the Penang version, because it uses dark soya sauce. In Penang, a few pork dishes like Tau Eu Bak use dark soya sauce.

We take a lot of these sauces for granted. Take Suan Yong Chor for example. *Suan* refers to the garlic, *yong* means 'brewed' or 'pickled' and the *chor* is vinegar. This sauce is part of the Penang Nonya food repertoire and Poh Piah Chnee (deep-fried poh piah) would not be the same without it.

Lor is another sauce which gives the name to Lor Mee. In Penang, *lor* is served with Lor Bak together with a chilli sauce. A similar dish in Singapore is called Ngoh Hiang, presumably referring to the ngoh hiang hoon (five spice powder) used in the preparation. Of course the best ngoh hiang hoon comes from Penang; it is finely ground from fresh Szechuan pepper, star anise, cinnamon, cloves and fennel, two of which – clove and pepper – are grown locally.

There is also the red tnee cheow and the black aw cheow both of which are thin pastes used in Poh Piah among other dishes. Tnee Cheow is sweet (tnee means sweet in Hokkien) and maroon red while aw cheow is salty and has a different texture from black soya sauce. Tnee cheow is one of the sauces used with heh ko (prawn paste) to mix with sliced fruits to make Penang Rojak.

Noodles of different thicknesses and cross-sections feature prominently in Penang hawker food. There are Hokkien mee (fresh yellow wheat noodles), mee sua (wheat vermicelli), bee hoon (rice vermicelli), tung hoon (bean vermicelli) and koay teow (flat rice noodles). What I find interesting is the choice and combination of noodles used in Penang hawker fare. When ordering dishes like Hokkien Mee, Kali Mee/Maifun and Hainanese Fried Bee Hoon/Mee in Penang, you could choose to have bee hoon or mee or the two together. The other noodles are not normally served together in a dish. In Singapore, if you order Hokkien Mee (we call that Hokkien Char in Penang) you get thick bee hoon as well; you do not have a choice! Similarly, if you order Char Koay Teow in Kuala Lumpur or Singapore, most stalls would use mee and koay teow. Seh Jit Mee (birthday noodles) also known as Lam Mee (page 69) is a dish cooked by the Penang Nonyas to celebrate birthdays. The pre-cooked yellow egg noodle used is commonly referred to in Penang markets as Hokkien mee but it is also referred to elsewhere as sek mee or cooked noodles.

Moi (rice porridge) is commonly served at breakfast with light soya sauce, fried kiam hu (salt fish of different varieties), groundnuts and kiam ark nooi (salted duck egg). I grew up in my maternal grandmother's house at the corner of Macalister Road and Lorong Susu and remember the porridge stall across the road that used to serve the trishaw peddlers. In my mind, I still have this picture of trishaw peddlers squatting on the benches eating their food. My *Ah koo chee* (cousin) and I used to cross the road to buy porridge and fried groundnuts. The *moi* was rather thin and watery. I remember that it was mixed with sweet potatoes which I understand is a common crop in Fujian Province. Sweet potatoes were added to make up the bulk due to shortage of rice during famine or war. Besides being served plain, *moi* is cooked with meat and other ingredients. We have Bak Moi (pork porridge), Kay Moi (chicken porridge) and Hu Moi (fish porridge), often served with Eu Char Koay (Chinese cruller – deep fried unsweetened dough shaped into twin

BAMBOO

Bamboo shoot harvested in spring, summer and winter are different from each other. Spring bamboo shoots are chunky and pale while winter shoots are daintier, more elongated, finer in texture and of a deeper colour. Summer bamboo shoots are pencil-thin and seldom available outside China.

There are numerous uses for the bamboo other than as food.

The leaves are used for wrapping Chang (dumplings), the bamboo for chopsticks and furniture such as stools. My cousin still has a multi-purpose bamboo chair which, when turned on its side, serves as a seat for feeding babies.

Various cooking utensils like *karlow* (col-

ander), satay sticks, baskets and trays ranging in size from the very small to the large *nyiru* (Malay tray) are all made of bamboo.

The *siah nah* commonly used by Nonyas for carrying food especially on auspicious occasions is a well-finished basket made of bamboo. The Hokkien *siah nah* is lacquered and painted while the Teochew version has bare bamboo. There is also a Hockchew version which is square or hexagonal and is also lacquered.

The Wanthan Mee hawkers used a small stick of bamboo to hit a larger piece to make the 'tok-tok' sound as they plied the streets of Penang, selling what we called Tok-Tok Mee.

Bamboo shoots locally grown in Penang.

My sister seated in a multi-purpose bamboo chair.

A Teochew bamboo siah nah.

*Hawker stalls clustered under trees at Lau Heok Hnui (Betel Leaves Estate)
in Pulau Tikus – Lengkok Burma.*

foot-long strips). There is a Bak Moi stall near my grandmother's house at the junction of Lorong Selamat. At this stall, you have a choice of *moi* (grainy Hokkien/Teochew porridge), *chok* (Cantonese porridge cooked till the rice grains have disintegrated), mee sua or bee hoon. Traditionally, we go on a *moi* diet when we are not well. There is a good reason for that – the body can better absorb the soft porridge. I understand this is common even among western cultures when other grains like wheat or barley are consumed as gruel.

Fujian is the largest bamboo growing area in China with 140 varieties in existence. This is why the bamboo shoot (soon) is an important ingredient in Hokkien cooking. It used to be the main ingredient of Ju Hu Char and the Poh Piah filling, but in Penang it has been largely replaced by bangkwang (yambean, also known as jicama) which is more readily available. Further, the preparation of the fresh bamboo shoots is rather tedious. In Singapore and Malacca, bamboo shoot is still a significant ingredient used together with bangkwang in Poh Piah and Koay Pai Ti.

Cloud ear fungus (*Tremella juciformis*) – the silver or white on called yin er and the black one called mo er – is in good supply in Fujian Province. White cloud ear fungus is used in a dessert called See Ko Thng, four ingredient soup (page 105). This dish is known as Cheng Thng in other parts of Malaysia and Singapore. *Cheng* refer to the cooling nature of the soup. Ingredients used in See Ko Thng are dried longan, lotus seeds, ginko nuts, dried lily buds, geta angul (a resin which when soaked in water expands into a colourless lump), phong tai hai (emas mangor – a dark brown, olive-shaped fruit which, when soaked in water, expands into a brown mass, lotus seeds, agar-agar, Chinese barley, preserved persimmons and preserved winter melon. We used to take this dessert in the evening at the hawker centre at the Esplanade. It was one of the earliest hawker centres in Penang, in the days when most hawkers plied the streets.

The transition from mobile street stalls to hawker centres began with hawkers clustering around coffee shops. A well-known *kopi tiam* cluster in my young days is the one 'next to Queens' as what my parents used to say. A better known hawker cluster to visitors to Penang today is the one in Gurney Drive, which is a recent development and not a heritage site! Other bigger hawker centres set up by private enterprises have proliferated in Penang. Although the Hokkiens account for a very high percentage of Chinese in Penang, there are very few Hokkien restaurants in Penang, compared with Cantonese or Hainanese ones. Ang Hoay Lor is one of the very few Hokkien establishments.

SNEH JIT MEE
LAM MEE
BIRTHDAY NOODLES

No birthday celebration in a Nonya family would be complete without Sneh Jit Mee. A prawn- and pork-based gravy is poured (*lam* in Hokkien) all over blanched Hokkien mee, beansprouts, and Chinese chives arranged on a plate. The dish is garnished with crab meat and roe, thin strips of thinly fried omelettes, fried shallots, spring onions and sliced chilies. The Sneh Jit Mee must be served with Sambal Belacan which is a Malay condiment. The noodles used for birthday mee is referred to in Penang as Hokkien mee. As it is pre-cooked, it is also known as sek (cooked) mee in Singapore.

Traditionally, the noodle is partaken in a meal to celebrate a birthday. A birthday meal must include noodles because the long strands of noodles signify long life, hence the noodles should not be cut when it is dished out. Everyone must have a bowl or at least a token mouthful during a birthday meal. The ingredients used have much significance. The beansprouts and coriander shoots signify rejuvenation while the chives signify perpetuality since the shoots of chives, when cut, will re-grow. The eggs in the dish denote fertility.

I have heard that a traditional mee sua (wheat vermicelli) dish is prepared for a celebratory breakfast and Hokkien Lam Mee for the lunch, but this is not the practice with my grandmother. In my pre-school days, I vaguely remember birthday noodles carried in a *sia nah* being distributed to close friends and relatives on my maternal grandmother, Tan Siew Kee's birthday. The recipient would transfer the noodles to another plate, wash the original plate and return it with a token of two eggs and bunch of mee sua wrapped in a strip of red paper. This practice is called *tnak puah* or 'weight on the plate' in Hokkien. The same red paper was used to wrap *ang pow* (red packet) as there were no ready-made envelopes in those days.

Belly pork is normally used but in some countries such as the UK, pork ribs are sold with the belly. In those cases, pork ribs can be used but not served formally.

Sneh Jit Mee
(Serves 12)

Gravy
400 g prawns
500 g belly pork
100 g shallots
5 cloves garlic
2 tbsp oil
3 tbsp light soya sauce
3 tbsp plain flour
2 tbsp sugar
3 tsp salt
3 litres water

Noodle & Garnishes
1.2 kg Hokkien mee
200g chives
500 g beansprouts
3 stalks spring onion
3 red chillies
2 crabs
3 eggs
Pinch of salt
3 stalks coriander leaves
Fried sliced shallots
Sambal Belacan (see page 39)

Gravy
Remove the heads of the prawns. Divide the prawns into two portions. Shell one portion of the prawns, de-vein and dice. De-vein the other portion of the prawns, but do not shell them, and set aside for garnishing. Keep the prawn head and shells aside for making the stock.

Put the prawn shells and heads with the belly pork in a sauce pan and fill it with enough water to cover the pork. Bring to a boil, lower the heat and simmer for about 15 to 20 minutes. The pork should not be overcooked. It is ready once the pink meat turns white. Remove the pork from the saucepan and keep the stock simmering.

Remove excess fat and the skin from the belly pork. Slice the pork thinly (about 2 mm) and then cut the slices into thin strips 2 mm wide.

Put the prawns with shells on into the boiling stock. Remove when the shells turn orange. Shell these prawns for garnishing. Put the shells you have just removed into the pot with the other prawn shells and simmer for another 5 minutes. Now strain the stock and set aside. Discard the prawn shells.

Peel the shallots and slice thinly; smash the garlic, remove the skin, and chop up finely. Fry the sliced shallot and chopped garlic in oil till nearly brown.

Add the diced prawns and salt, 1 tablespoon of the light soya sauce and fry till the prawns begin to turn pink. Include the pork strips and fry till some lard comes off the fat. Now put in the rest of the light soya sauce, sugar and the stock. Add 3 litres of water. Simmer for 30 minutes. Set aside.

Noodles & Garnishes
Cut the chive into lengths of about 3 cm. Wash the beansprouts and nip off the root ends if labour is available! Slice the spring onions finely. Remove the seeds from the chillies and slice the chillies thinly at a diagonal.

Steam the crabs and pick out the meat.

Boil enough water to cover the chives. Prepare another pot of cold water. Quickly blanch the chives and plunge in cold water. The chive loses its colour and texture if overcooked.

Blanch the beansprouts for about half a minute. Rinse in cold water, drain and keep aside.

Boil a fresh, large pot of water. Put in the noodles and remove the pot from the fire just before the water boils again (about 2 minutes). The Hokkien mee is already pre-cooked so it should not be overcooked. Drain and wash the noodles liberally with cold water to ensure that they do not stick together. Blanch the noodles in two batches if a large pot is not available.

Beat the egg and add the pinch of salt. Traditionally, a bit of red food colouring is added to obtain a pink omelette. Heat up a pan and liberally wipe it with tissue infused with oil. Pour sufficient beaten egg into the pan and swivel to make a thin omelette. Remove before the egg turns brown. Roll up the omelette and slice thinly (about 1 mm). Set aside for garnish.

Serving
Render the plain flour with a little water and pour into the boiling gravy to slightly thicken it just before serving.

This is how the birthday noodle is presented: The chives are spread on a large shallow bowl and the beansprouts are spread over the chives. The noodles are placed over the bean sprouts.

The gravy is poured (*lam*) over the noodles. Arrange the whole prawns, crab meat and roe, sliced omelette, fried shallots, spring onions, coriander leaves and finally the slice chillies, in that order, on the noodles.

Serve with Sambal Belacan and keat lah. To the Penang Nonya, Sneh Jit Mee will not taste right without this condiment.

Birthday parties at home in the 1960s. The tea and buffet tables were laden with lovingly prepared home-made savory and sweet dishes.

POH PIAH, POH PIAH CHNEE & MAMAK POH PIAH

Poh Piah means 'thin biscuit' in Hokkien, referring to the thin Poh Piah skin. It is a Hokkien dish made up of a filling based on shredded vegetables and several garnishes and condiments, all wrapped up into a cylindrical roll in the thin crepe-like skin. It is a popular Penang hawker dish but is often served at home where family members and friends can wrap their own Poh Piah, adding and leaving out whatever they wish.

The filling for Poh Piah is similar to that for Koay Pai Ti (page 85) and Ju Hu Char (page 89). The original filling is mainly bamboo shoots, which is plentiful in Fujien Province. In Penang, and more so in Singapore, home-cooked versions still use a large proportion of bamboo shoots in the filling. However, hawkers have replaced bamboo shoots with the readily available and convenient bangkwang (also known as huan kuak, jicama and yambean).

Bamboo shoots do not feature prominently in the Poh Piah filling prepared by our close relatives in Penang on both my father and my mother's sides of the family, except in my see ee's (fourth aunt's) household. My see teow's (uncle's) Singapore influence must have predominated in their food preference probably because my see ee does not cook.

The Poh Piah filling consists of bangkwang, French beans and some carrots. The last ingredient was introduced in recent times. My mother had always used French beans in her Poh Piah filling. We used carrots, tinned bamboo shoots and cabbage in London in the 1970s because bangkwang was not readily available there at the time. It is ironic; we have gone a full circle – Poh Piah started using mainly bamboo shoots which

were replaced by bangkwang in Penang and now, since bangkwang is not so readily available in some places, we are going back to using tinned bamboo shoots.

The vegetables are finely shredded into juliennes with a sharp knife. This is the method preferred by the traditional Nonyas as the shreds will be of a uniform shape and size. Various tools are also used for shredding the bangkwang. The old shredder was a perforated brass sheet mounted on a wooden block. It produced irregular shreds that were mushy even before they were cooked. A good tool is the mandoline which employs two sets of blades at right angles to each other. It has changable blades of different sizes to cut juliennes of various widths. The shreds come out regular and fine if the small blades are employed. I am very impressed and I am sure the traditional Nonya would approve the use of the mandoline for shredding. My cousin, who used to cut Poh Piah filling by hand, has switched to the mandoline – a strong endorsement from someone who still grinds her spices using a *batu giling* (stone mill). However, you need some muscle power to use the mandoline effectively. Labour saving devices are important in the preparation of Poh Piah since there is a lot of shredding to be done for a Poh Piah party. Today, many manual and electrical food processors have shredders incorporated in their designs.

The Poh Piah filling from Penang does not include tau chiow (fermented soya beans) and hardly uses Chinese sausage, sliced fried egg or pounded peanut as garnishes. The key garnishes are fried sliced shallot and the fried shredded tau kwa (firm soya bean cake). The shredded tau kwa could be added to the main filling but it is not done in our family because the fillings tend to go sour faster if the *tau kwa* is included. It is shredded belly pork and prawns that give the filling its taste.

There are two types of skins used to wrap Poh Piah – the original Hokkien ones that we buy and the homemade Nonya ones which are similar to crepes. The thicker Nonya Poh Piah skins are not popular in Penang probably because locally-made Hokkien ones are readily available and inexpensive. My mother only makes the skin for Choon Piah, a related dish. Poh Piah skins are made in different sizes – the large ones are about 25 cm in diameter and the small ones, approximately 15 cm in diameter. Factory-made Poh Piah skins are now widely available. They come in frozen packs. Personally, I do not like them for Poh Piah as I find them too much like plastic, but they are great for Poh Piah Chnee (page 73). My wife uses them for making samosas (page 164).

Left-over Poh Piah filling is traditionally used to make Poh Piah Chnee which are deep fried small Poh Piah. This is one of the items sold by the Indian *kuih* men who plied the streets of Penang. This, however, is not Mamak Poh Piah (see page 83), which is an Indian variation characterized by its spicy sweet and sour sauce.

Today, Poh Piah Chnee is a popular cocktail finger food in Malaysia and in Singapore.

A Mamak Poh Piah stall.

Poh Piah
(Makes 12 rolls)

500 g Poh Piah skin

Filling
1 kg bangkwang (yambean, also known as jicama)
300 g French beans
400 g prawns
400 g belly pork
4 cloves garlic
1 tbsp oil
1 tsp salt

Garnishes
600 g crabs
300 g tau kwa (firm soya bean cake)
1 large cucumber
300 g local lettuce
300 g beansprouts
50 g fried chopped garlic
150 g fried sliced shallot
2 tbsp oil (for frying tau kwa)

Condiments
150 g fresh red chilies
100 g garlic
Tnee cheow (sweet red thin pasty sauce)
Aw cheow (a black, salty and thin pasty sauce)

Filling
Julienne the bangkwang into sticks of about 3 x 3 mm and 5 to 6 cm long or shred using a mandoline. Slice the French beans thinly on the slant so that each piece is about 15 mm long. This is how the Nonya sliced them.

Peel the prawns and de-vein and dice; keep the prawn heads and shells aside for stock.

Put the prawn shells and heads with the belly pork in a pot and add enough water to cover the pork. Bring to a boil, lower the fire, and simmer for about 15 minutes. The pork should not be overcooked. It is ready once the meat turns greyish. Remove the belly pork. Discard the prawn shells and heads. Keep the stock for use later.

Cut off the skin from the belly pork and remove the excess fat if the belly pork is too fatty. Cut the pork thinly into 2 mm slices. Then cut across the slices to obtain strips of about 2 mm in thickness.

Skin the garlic and chop up finely. Heat 1 tbsp of oil in a pan. When the oil is hot, fry the chopped garlic till it is nearly brown. Add the diced prawns and 1 tsp salt and fry till the prawns are cooked. Include the pork strips and fry till some lard comes off the pork. Now put in the bangkwang and fry for about 5 minutes. Add the stock gradually and allow to simmer on a low fire for at least 30 minutes. Put in the French beans towards the end of the cooking time and fry till it changes from light to dark green.

Drain as much of the gravy as possible and reserve the gravy for making Poh Piah.

Garnishes
Steam the crabs and, when cooked, separate the flesh from the shell. Set the flesh aside.

Slice the tau kwa into pieces of about 2 mm thickness and then cut into 2 mm-strips. Heat 2 tbsp of oil in a pan and, when the oil is hot, fry the tau kwa strips until just light brown. Drain the oil and keep this garnish aside.

Cut off the ends of the cucumber. Skin the cucumber and slice it lengthwise into quarters. Remove the core and cut each piece of cucumber into two or three, lengthwise. Then cut in lengths of about 6 cm.

Wash the lettuce and separate the leaves from the stalk. Remove most of the thick stalk of the leaves.

Traditionally, the roots of the beansprouts are nipped so the sprouts look neater, but we may not have time for such luxury today. Wash and then blanch the beansprouts in the boiling water. Drain.

Prepare fried sliced shalllot and fried chopped garlic.

Condiments
Rinse the chillies, remove the stalks and slit them open lengthwise. Remove the seeds and pound the chillies in a mortar or grind in a food processor. Set aside.

Skin the garlic cloves, smash them and pound in a mortar or grind in a food processor. Set aside.

Pour the tnee cheow and aw cheow into separate small bowls.

My paternal aunt Nell standing next to an old oven. We had one similar to it in our kitchen at home.

Making Poh Piah

Arrange the following on a table: The Poh Piah skins wrapped in a damp cloth to keep them moist and pliable, the filling, a bowl of the reserved gravy, the garnishes and the condiments. Each diner should have a plate big enough to contain the Poh Piah skin and a sharp knife for slicing the finished Poh Piah.

Spread the Poh Piah skin on a plate. Place a lettuce leaf off-centre on the skin, nearer you. In my family, we use a stick of cucumber to spread the condiments: sweet tnee cheow, salty aw cheow, hot ground chillies and ground garlic, all according to personal preference. The back of a teaspoon can also be used effectively to spread the condiments. If you like your Poh Piah pristine white, spread your condiments on the lettuce leaf.

Drain the bravy from the Poh Piah filling. This is to ensure that the Poh Piah skin stays as dry as possible, otherwise you will end up with a soggy, punctured Poh Piah, with the filling spilling onto the plate. You could place an inverted bowl in a large container and pile the Poh Piah filling on the bowl so that the gravy drains away. Otherwise, you can use the backs of two serving spoons to press and drain the filling of excess gravy as you make each Poh Piah.

Place the filling along the length of the lettuce leaf. Add the beansprouts, fried tau kwa, crab meat, the fried shallot and fried chopped garlic. Put the cucumber sticks on this filling.

Fold the skin at the ends of the lettuce leaf inwards and, starting from the edge near you, roll the skin over the filling and garnishes, forming a tight cylindrical shape.

The proper way to eat the Poh Piah is to use a sharp knife to slice the spring roll into 2 to 3 cm pieces. A really sharp knife is needed, otherwise the Poh Piah would end up in a mess. Moisten the Poh Piah with a few spoonful of the reserved gravy to soften the skin. This is how Poh Piah is served in Penang. Others prefer to eat Poh Piah in a not so elegant manner by picking the whole roll up and biting a mouthful at a time. You can identify a Penangite by the way he eats his Poh Piah. In Singapore, Poh Piah is eaten dry.

The larger skins are usually used to make Poh Piah at home. The smaller skins are used by hawkers who normally use two small overlapping skins for each Poh Piah. The smaller Poh Piah skins are also used for Poh Piah Chnee which traditionally uses left-over filling with the tau kwa, but without the other garnishes or condiments.

Poh Piah at Padang Brown Hawker Centre, one of the earliest in Penang.

Poh Piah Skin

It is fascinating to watch poh piah phoey (skin) being made. There is a shop at Lebuh Chowrasta, next to the Chowrasta market, where the skins come hot off the pan. It all seems so easy and fast. For those interested in making your own Poh Piah skin, I strongly recommend that you visit this stall or your local Poh Piah skin store to carefully observe how the dough is so deftly wiped over the pan to yield this round, thin skin.

I saw Poh Piah skins being made years ago at shops in Carnervon Street and at the Penang Road and Bertam Lane junction. I then tried it out using the hot plate of the electric cooker at home and it worked!

My immediate family made our own Poh Piah skins in London. My *jee kor* (second aunt), though a good cook, did not quite get the hang of making the skins, and has been known to turn up with her bowl of Poh Piah skin dough to ask me to carry on where she had left off.

1 kg strong flour*
1 litre water
1 tsp salt

* Strong flour is high in protein and gluten content.

Sieve the flour into a cake mixer or food processor with a dough hook attachment, add the salt and then, slowly, 700 ml of the water. The dough will form a lump and separate from the sides of the bowl when it is ready. If you are using a small food processor, mix the dough in two or three batches.

Alternatively, knead like a dough mix. Sieve the flour on a work-top, make a well in the flour, add water in the well and slowly mix the flour with the water. Knead the dough until the dough forms a lump which does not stick to the work-top or your hand.

Add 100 ml of water and mix.

Cover the dough with a damp cloth and leave aside for 3 to 4 hours or overnight in the fridge. If the latter, let the dough warm up to room temperature before using.

When you are ready to make the Poh Piah skin, add about 75 ml water into the dough and mix until it becomes more pliable.

Pour 125 ml of water into a bowl and add an equal volume of the dough to form a thin watery paste. Pour this watery mixture into a large bowl and put the rest of the dough in it. This watery paste at the bottom of the bowl will keep the working dough moist.

Heat up a heavy cast iron griddle or a thick flat frying pan and keep on low heat. Getting the right temperature is best done by trial and error. The temperature is too high if the skin is slightly brown.

At this stage, mix the dough with your dominant hand. Lift a handful of the dough, sufficient to cover the hand like a boxing glove. Move the arm, the hand, wrist and fingers to ensure that the whole lump of dough stays together around the hand. This is best achieved by moving the lower arm in a circular motion and the hand also in a circular motion at the wrist. A lot of practice is needed to keep the dough together in a ball and to be able to control the movement of the dough.

Quickly wipe the dough in a circular motion over the griddle to form a round skin. If the pan is too hot the skin will come off the pan and will still be stuck to the dough. It is critical that the dough is well kneaded, otherwise the skin will not come off the pan easily.

There may be some areas on the skin which has more dough. This can be picked up by quickly re-touching the area with the dough in the hand. You can also use a scraper to spread out the dough. The Poh Piah skin will separate from the griddle, starting from the edge. Lift the skin from the griddle before it turns brown. At this stage the skin is rather crispy. Stack the skins as you make them. They will soften.

Dip the dough in your hand into the liquid mixture every ten minutes or when required to keep it wet and continue the circular motion described earlier. Occasionally remix the dough in the hand with the rest in the bowl.

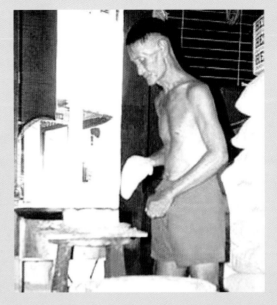

The late Ong Boon Cheng., He is the patriach of the Ong family in Lebuh Tye Sin (otherwise known as 'See Tiao Lor' or 4th street by locals) which has been producing popiah skin for the past six decades.

Poh Piah skin is made by wiping the dough on the hot gridle. It looks so easy!

Now a popular finger food at cocktail parties, Poh Piah Chnee used to sold by Indian kuih men who also sold Nonya kuih and Nonya Laksa on the streets of Penang.

Poh Piah Chnee

At home, leftover Poh Piah filling is not wasted. It is traditionally used to make Poh Piah Chnee (deep fried Poh Piah). The smaller Poh Piah skin is used for wrapping.

Poh Piah Chnee are about 12 cm long. In recent times, those served as finger food are smaller. There are now also factory-made Poh Piah skins which are more suitable for Poh Piah Chnee than for Poh Piah. They come in frozen packs, made in Singapore, the US and Canada, and are available world-wide.

Poh Piah Chnee is served with Suan Yong Chor (page 64). However, the condiments and garnishes for Poh Piah are not used for the traditional Poh Piah Chnee except for the tau kwa.

If you like your Poh Piah Chnee crispy and you are not particular about the amount of filling in it, you could wrap the Poh Piah Chnee twice with two separate layers of skin.

Poh Piah Chnee is related to Spring Roll or Choon Piah which has quite a different filling of minced meat, crab meat, mushrooms onions and other vegetables.

Mamak Poh Piah

This is a *mamak* (Indian Muslim) hawker version of the Hokkien/Nonya Poh Piah. All the ingredients used for this dish are *halal*. It uses the basic Poh Piah ingredients of bangkwang, prawns, soyabean cake, beansprouts and fried shallots, but without the other garnishes and condiments. The most distinguishing feature of this Poh Piah is the sauce, concocted by *mamak* using local ingredients like tamarind, dried chillies and onions. The tamarind (assam Jawa in Malay) gives the sauce its sour taste while raisins and dates provide a distinctive, sweet note. This unique sweet, sour and spicy sauce is so different from the condiments used in the Penang Poh Piah. This is an early example of the evolution of Nonya fusion food into *halal* food. More recently, *halal* versions of Nonya and Chinese dishes have become popular.

Mamak Poh Piah can be found at a stall on the Johor Road side of Padang Brown and also at another stall in Swatow Lane. There are similar versions in Singapore – one stall is at Kadang Kerbau Market – but these are more similar to the Nonya version.

Mamak Poh Piah normally uses the smaller Poh Piah skins. The Poh Piah is sliced into 4 or 5 pieces. Some gravy from the filling is drizzled over before the *mamak* gravy is spread on. The filling is a simplified version of the Nonya one. It is made up mainly of bangkwang and not a lot of prawns. Long beans are sometimes used instead of French beans, but they are not cut as finely. The Mamak Poh Piah filling has a tint of yellow because of the ground turmeric added. The garnishes are mashed fried tau kwa and beansprouts. Some stalls also use lettuce and fried sliced shallots.

The simplified version of this Poh Piah filling uses yambeans and prawns, replacing the French beans with long beans. One teaspoon of ground turmeric is added to give the filling a tinge of yellow. The condiments are replaced by the Mamak Poh Piah sauce. The only garnishes used are fried tau kwa, blanched bean sprouts and fried sliced shallots.

Sauce

50 g raisins
50 g dates
2 tsp chilli powder
½ tbsp assam (tamarind), seeds removed
30 ml warm water for tamarind
200 ml water
50 g shallots
½ tsp salt
1½ tsp sugar
1 tbsp oil

Break up the tamarind into smaller pieces and soak them in the 30 ml of warm water. When the tamarind pulp has softened, remove any stray seeds and squeeze the tamarind between the thumb and fingers to separate the pulp from the fibres. Use a strainer to separate the liquid from the fibre.

Remove the seeds from the dates and stalks from the raisins

Mix the chilli powder with 2 tsp of water into a paste.

Peel the shallots and slice thinly. Heat the tablespoon of oil in a pan and fry the sliced onions till slightly brown. Remove from the oil and set aside.

Fry the chilli paste till it is fragrant.

Blend the chillies, fried shallots, dates and raisins together in a food processor. Transfer to a saucepan, add the water, tamarind liquid, salt and sugar, and bring to the boil. Simmer for 5 minutes.

Serve the sause warm.

KOAY PAI TI

This recipe is based on my mother's original compiled in the 1950s when she gave demonstrations to her fellow YWCA members in Penang. Koay Pai Ti may have originated from Singapore. It was also called Singapore Poh Piah and I have read that it was also known as Syonanto Pie, Syonanto being the name of Singapore during the Japanese Occupation. The 'pie' may explain the origin of the 'pai' in Pai Ti. There is an Indonesian dish known as Java Kwei Patti or Kroket Tjanker, which uses the same Pai Ti shells. Aunty Jane from my wife's side of the family used Min Chee (see page 121) – a mixture of diced meat, potatoes, carrots and peas – as a filling instead. I then realised that this is a related dish which has Dutch origins.

Koay Pai Ti is an attractive Nonya *hors d'oeuvre* of Pai Ti shells filled with a filling similar to that of Poh Piah – but that's where the association ends. In my mother's Pai Ti, the vegetables for the filling are drier and just cooked; it should be still crunchy, unlike the Pai Ti filling which is wet and soggy. There is a good practical reason for that; it is to ensure that the Pai Ti shells stay crispy before it is consumed. If the Pai Ti shells are not too big, the whole Pai Ti can be elegantly eaten in one mouthful.

Most of the Pai Ti that I have come across, especially in Singapore, uses Poh Piah filling. My wife made Pai Ti for a YWCA funfair in Singapore many years ago. There was another Pai Ti stall, but my wife's Pai Ti was very quickly sold out – well before the other stall's.

Diced, boiled prawns can be used for garnishing, but as Penang food is not ostentatious, this is not commonly seen.

The Pai Ti shell is made by dipping a hot brass mould in a batter. A layer of the batter forms on the side of the mould which is then immersed into hot oil. The batter is pliable before it cooks, so a variety of shapes for the shell can be obtained by careful manipulation of the mould in the oil. If the mould is moved up and down, a top hat-shaped shell will emerge. The Pai Ti shell will detach itself from the mould when the batter hardens into a crusty shell. If the mould is removed from the oil before the batter hardens, the shell will fold up like a clam!

Pai Ti moulds are more readily available today. It was difficult to buy one in the 1950s, so my father had to commission a blacksmith to make them.

The following ingredients are sufficient for making about 100 Pai Ti shells. This is about the optimum minimum amount to make, bearing in mind that some of the batter at the end has to be discarded because a minimum depth of batter is required for dipping in the mould. Therefore, it is best to put the batter into a tall cup with a small opening.

Pai Ti Shells
(Makes about 100)

70 g wheat flour
100 g ground rice flour
1½ tbsp cornflour
1 egg
1 tsp oil
280 ml water
Pinch of salt
Pinch of pepper
Pinch of kapur (slaked lime)
Oil for deep frying

Sieve the wheat flour, ground rice flour and tapioca flour together. Beat the egg and mix with the flour mixture. Add the oil and continue stirring. Water should be added gradually as you stir to obtain a consistent thick, liquid paste. If too much water is added at once it becomes difficult to get rid of the lumps that form. The batter becomes thinner as more water is added. Alternatively, the mixture could be mixed altogether in a food processor. Set aside for an hour before making shells.

Heat oil in a deep pan for deep frying and heat the Pai Ti mould in the oil till the mould is hot. Dip the hot mould in the batter. Do not totally immerse the mould; leave a gap of ½ cm from the top of the mould.

Immerse the batter-coated mould in the hot oil. Note that the oil is too hot if the batter bubbles when it is immersed. For a standard-shaped Pai Ti shell, keep the mould steady. For a top-hat-shaped shell, move the mould vertically up and down while the batter is flexible. If the vertical motion is excessive the shell will detach from the mould before the shell has hardened, giving rise to a distorted shell.

When the batter has hardened, the shell will detach itself from the mould. If it does not slip off, use a satay stick to ease the shell from the mould. Remove the shell from the oil when it is light brown; remember it will continue browning even after it has been removed from the oil. Allow to drain on kitchen paper. Keep in an airtight container.

NOTE: The behaviour of the batter – whether the shell comes off easily from the mould or whether you can make the hat-shaped shell depends very much on the flour used and the temperature of the oil (about 200° C). In general the first few shells tend to stick to the mould.

Pai Ti Filling
(For about 100 shells)

1.2 kg bangkwang (yambean, also known as jicama)
200 g bamboo shoots (optional)
300 g carrots
300 g French beans
10 stalks spring onions
4 crabs
600 g prawns
600 g belly pork
400 g tau kwa (firm soyabean cake)
4 cloves garlic
6 tbsp oil
2 tsp salt

Reduce bangkwang by 200 g if bamboo shoots are used.

Cut the bangkwang and carrots into fine sticks about 2 to 3 cm long, or shred using a mandoline. Slice the French beans thinly on the slant. Chop up the spring onions and set aside for garnishing.

Steam the crabs and separate the flesh from the shells.

Peel the prawns, de-vein and dice; keep the prawn heads and shells aside for the stock.

Put the prawn shells and heads with the belly pork in a pot and add enough water to cover the pork. Bring to a boil, lower the fire and simmer for about 15 minutes. The pork should not be overcooked. It is ready once the meat turns greyish. Remove the belly pork. Discard the prawn shells and heads. Keep the stock for use later.

Remove the skin from the belly pork and the excess fat also if the belly pork is too fatty. Cut the pork thinly into 2 mm slices. Then cut into across the slices to obtain strips of about 2 mm thickness.

Slice the tau kwa into pieces of about 2 mm thickness and then cut into 2 mm-strips. Heat the frying pan till hot then add the 6 tbsp of oil and fry the tau kwa strips until they turn light brown. Drain and keep aside.

Skin the garlic and chop them up finely. Heat the oil used for the tau kwa in a pan. When the oil is hot, fry the chopped garlic till they are nearly brown. Add the diced prawns and the salt and fry till the prawns are cooked. Include the pork strips and fry till some lard comes off the pork.

Now put in the carrots and fry for 2 minutes. Add the bangkwang and fry for a further 3 minutes. Include the beans toward the end of the cooking time and fry till it changes from light to dark green. Finally, add the fried tau kwa and stir thoroughly.

Small amounts of stock can be added during the frying if the mixture is too dry. If too much stock is added, the mixture will become too wet. The general idea is to fry the vegetables till they are just cooked so that they are remain crunchy.

Pai Ti Sauce
(Makes about 150 ml)

3 large fresh chillies (about 50 g)
60 g peanuts
2 tsp sugar
½ tsp salt
130 ml water
2 tsp vinegar (best to use natural vinegar)
1 tbsp sesame seeds, toasted

Rinse the chillies. Remove the stalks, slit open and discard the seeds. Grind or pound the chillies finely. Pound the peanuts finely.

Mix the ground chillies, peanuts, sugar, and salt with the water. Add vinegar to taste. Sprinkle on the toasted sesame seeds before serving.

Serving the Pai Ti
Fill the Pai Ti shells with the filling and top with the crabmeat and chopped spring onions. Serve with the chillie sauce. Fried sliced shallots could also be added as garnishing.

The Pai Ti shells will turn soggy if the Pai Ti is not consumed quickly.

JU HU CHAR

Ju Hu Char, literally translated from Hokkien, is 'cuttlefish fried'. In this context, *char* means 'dish'. Ju Hu Char is a Penang variant of a Hokkien dish based on finely shredded vegetables, mainly *bangkwang* (yambean) and onions, fried with shredded pork and dried thinly sliced cuttlefish. Carrots were added in more recent times to give the dish a dash of colour. Although Ju Hu Char is also served at day-to-day meals, it is one of several traditional Penang Nonya dishes prepared for special occasions.

Ju Hu Char is served with other festive dishes like Pnee Hu (dried sole) Char, Hu Chi (shark's fin) Char and Kiam Chai Ark Thng (Salted Vegetable and Duck Soup). Among the Penang Nonya, the dish features in reunion dinners on Chinese New Year's eve, feasts for traditional weddings, funerals and important birthdays as well as offerings at *cheng beng* (Chinese All Souls Day) and at anniversaries in remembrance of the departed.

For important occasions like weddings, the food was prepared in the past by a Hainanese chef (*cham phor*) who was engaged months in advance to cook for the occasion. He would come the night before the event with his apprentice and all their cooking utensils, but the crockery and cutlery would be provided by the family. The ingredients for the feast were bought by the host from a long list given by the chef or it could be supplied by the chef at cost. The *cham phor* did all the cooking outside the house under a tarpaulin. I was impressed that the *cham phor* could get by with only two cleavers. He didn't need a can opener; he could open cans with his chopper.

Ju Hu Char, left-over from a feast, improves the taste of a Penang Nonya speciality called Kiam Chai Boey. It is a potpourri of left-over food. What remains of the vegetables, the soups, the chicken, the duck, roast pork, except curries and spicy food are gathered together in a large pot and cooked with kiam chai (salted vegetables). That is why it is called Kiam Chai Boey, as *boey* in Hokkien means 'end', being what remains of the feast. We all looked forward to the Kiam Chai Boey, especially if suckling pig had been served; if not, we added some roast pork. Likewise, if there wasn't much Ju Hu Char left over we would add sliced bangkwang, cabbage, carrots, baby sweet corn and bamboo shoots.

It is best to use cabbage with thinner leaves for this dish. The cabbage with thicker leaves and stems are a little bitter if they are not well cooked. If you have no choice, remove the thick stalk and only use the leaves.

If bangkwang is not available, use bamboo shoots and increase the proportions of carrots and cabbage. Shredded leek can also be added. If the shredded ju hu is not available, use dried cuttlefish and slice it yourself.

Some families include tow chneoh (preserved salted soya beans) in their recipe but, in general, tow chneoh is not so commonly used in Penang Nonya food compared with those from Malacca or Singapore.

Tok Panjang wedding dinner of my Uncle Joe and Aunty Kay at our Tanjong Tokong house.

Ju Hu Char

(Serves 12 with other dishes)

50 g dried ju hu (cuttlefish), shredded
300 g belly pork
600 g bangkwang (yambean, also known as jicama)
100 g carrots
150 g cabbage
120 g onions
25 g dried Chinese mushrooms
1 tsp white vinegar
3 cloves garlic
2 shallots
3 tbsp oil
1½ tbsp light soya sauce
500 ml water
1 tsp salt

Garnishes & Condiments
Spring onions, sliced at a slant, about 2 to 3 cm long
Kin chai (Chinese celery), chopped
Lettuce (about 20 leaves)
Sambal Belacan (page 39)

Put the belly pork in a pot and add enough water to cover the pork. Bring to a boil, lower the fire and simmer for about 15 minutes. The pork should not be overcooked. It is ready once the meat turns greyish. Remove the belly pork. Keep the stock for use later.

Cut off the skin from the belly pork and remove the excess fat if the belly pork is too fatty. Cut the pork thinly into 2 mm slices. Then cut across the slices to obtain strips of about 2 mm in thickness.

Julienne the bangkwang into sticks of about 2 x 2 mm and about 5 cm long or shred using a mandoline. The carrots are similarly shredded. Note that the shreds are finer for this dish compared to the Poh Piah filling.

Stack up several cabbage leaves together and slice thinly (about 1 mm wide). Peel the onions, cut away the root ends and slice each onion into two through the base. Slice the onions from the base to the tip.

Choose smaller and thinner mushrooms so that they are about the same size as the shredded vegetables when they are sliced. Soak the mushrooms in water for about 30 minutes and cut away the stems.

Soak the shredded ju hu in water with 1 tsp of vinegar for about 10 minutes. Drain.

Peel the garlic, smash and chop them up finely. Peel the shallots and slice thinly.

Heat a wok. Add the oil and when the oil is hot, fry the ju hu till it crackles and pops. Drain the oil and keep the ju hu aside.

Fry the garlic and the shallots in another tablespoon of oil. Stir continuously, otherwise you will end up with burnt garlic. Add the shredded pork with the salt and fry till some lard comes off the fat of the pork. Add the mushrooms and light soya sauce, stirring continuously. Add sliced onions and then the carrot, the bangkwang and the cabbage in that order, a little at a time. Stir continuously. If the mixture is too dry, add the stock from the boiled belly pork, again, a little at a time.

Finally add the fried ju hu and simmer for about 10 minutes.

Garnish with sliced spring onions and Chinese celery.

Ju Hu Char is traditionally served on a bed of Chinese lettuce leaves together with Sambal Belacan.

TAU EU BAK

(Serves 12 with other dishes)

Tau Eu Bak is a popular Hokkien dish served by many Chinese families in Penang. Tau eu is dark soya sauce and bak refers to the meat used in this dish. Belly pork or *sam chan* is traditionally used. It is a relatively simple dish to cook, using basic ingredients of Chinese cooking like dark soya sauce, garlic, peppercorn, egg and sugar. In the past, fried firm soyabean cake (tau kwa) was added – most probably to add bulk to the dish, since we did not eat so much meat in those days.

The *tau kwa* is normally cut up into smaller pieces and shallow fried, providing a seal for each piece of the soya bean cake. It can also be fried whole then cut up into smaller pieces so that they soak up the gravy.

Tau Eu Bak goes well with rice because of the generous amount of gravy. Like many Penang dishes, it tastes even better if served the day after it is cooked.

500 g belly pork
300 g tau kwa (firm soyabean cake)
2 tsp cooking oil
20 whole peppercorns
6 cloves garlic, smashed, skin on with side of chopper
2 tsp sugar
8 tbsp aw tau eu (black soya sauce)
150 ml water
2 eggs, hard-boiled and peeled
½ tsp salt or to taste

Cut the belly pork into 1½ to 2 cm slices. Traditionally, the skin of the belly pork is left on. For a healthier option, trim away some of the fat. It is important to dry the meat before cooking or the sauce will become cloudy.

Wash the tau kwa, dry with tissue and cut into cubes. Heat a wok till hot, then add the oil and shallow fry the tau kwa till slightly crispy. Keep aside.

Reheat the oil. Add the peppercorn and fry for about a minute (the peppercorn will break up if fried for too long). Include the garlic and continue frying and spreading the oil evenly around the saucepan, especially the sides, to ensure that the meat will not stick to the pan later.

Just when the garlic skin turns slightly brown, add the sugar and stir quickly for less than a minute. When it caramelizes, add the pork and fry for about 2 minutes, stirring constantly to ensure that the meat does not stick to the pan.

Add the black soya sauce and the water and simmer on low heat for about 30 minutes. Add the hard-boiled eggs and the fried tau kwa before serving. If you prefer, include the tau kwa earlier so that it will soak up some of the sauce.

Add salt to taste, as the amount of salt in the black soya sauce depends on the brand and quality used.

Tau Eu Bak is commonly served with Sambal Belacan.

LOR BAK & HEH CHNEE

Lor Bak is made by marinating strips of meat with five-spice powder (ngoh hiang hoon), soya sauce, among other ingredients, and rolling the meat in a beancurd skin or tau phoi. It is then deep fried. Many recipes use minced meat, but the hawker version and my mother's recipe uses strips of pork.

The *lor*, which gives the dish its name, is a starchy sauce made from stock, soya sauce and five-spice powder. Egg white is stirred in to give this brown sauce its characteristic white streaks. *Bak* is 'meat' in Hokkien.

As a hawker food, Lor Bak is served with other appetizers in a platter, the main ones being prawn fritters (Heh Chnee) and soya bean cake (tau kwa). Items which are also traditionally served include Sting Ray (Ikan Pari), boiled eggs, century eggs and cucumber wedges. Boiled pig ears and squid are sometimes served as well. These foods are cut into bite-size pieces and dipped into two condiments – the *lor* and the special chilli sauce – before eating. Hair pins were used in the old days for serving Lor Bak, but they have now been replaced with bamboo picks. It is a pity because I find it a bit fiddily when dipping my Heh Chnee or tow kwa pieces into the sauces using a single point bamboo pick. With the hairpin, which has two points, I can manoeuvre my food to completely coat it with the sauces.

There are two good places to eat Lor Bak – off Penang Road at Kampong Malabar and Sri Bahari Road. I think the prawn fritters at the Kampong Malabar Lor Bak stall is the best. It is crispy, doesn't have too much batter, and you can taste the prawns. You order any number of appetizers that you like at the hawker stalls. There is no standard order. Good Lor Bak was served by one of the many hawker stalls at a well-known Penang *kopi tiam* at the junction of Penang Road and Dicken Street, next to the old Queen's Theatre. Sadly, this heritage *kopi tiam* is no longer there. There is another variation of Lor Bak which can be found at a hawker stall at the junction of Malay Street and Carnavon Street. You have to go early because it sells out quickly. Here, marinated belly pork is deep fried without the beancurd sheets. At home and in Hainanese restaurants, Lor Bak is normally served with cucumber wedges as a dish but without the *lor* or Heh Chnee.

There is something similar to the Penang Lor Bak platter in Singapore. The Singapore vesion of Lor Bak is known as Ngoh Hiang, named after the five-spice powder, and minced pork is generally used. It sometimes finds its way into cold appetiser platters in restaurants. I have not seen the Singapore version served with *lor*.

They say that it is difficult to make *lor*. I went to London to study engineering and learned to make *lor*. I worked for many years in Holborn. I moonlighted and studied to make *lor*! My mother explained to me how *lor* is made but I have never seen her prepare it before. I learned to make *lor* by trial and error. This recipe is based on my mother's.

Lor Bak

(Makes 15 rolls)

400 g shoulder pork (*twee bak*), including skin
1 onion (approx. 60 g)
5 water chestnuts
1 egg
2 tsp five spice powder
1 tsp ground pepper
4 tsp light soya sauce
1 tbsp sugar
3 tbsp sweet potato flour
  (use tapioca flour or cornflour if unavailable)
1 large sheet beancurd skin
Oil for deep frying

Lor

300 ml chicken or pork stock
5 tsp cornflour or tapioca flour
1 tsp five-spice powder
1 tbsp sugar
3 tbsp light soya sauce
White from 1 egg

Lor Bak

Separate the lean meat from the fat. Slice the lean meat into strips about 1 x 1 x 7 cm. Slice the fat into strips about ½ x ½ x 7 cm. Peel the onions and chop up finely. Peel the water chestnuts and chop up finely.

Separate the yolk and white of the egg. Thoroughly mix the meat and fat with the egg yolk, five-spice powder, ground pepper, light soya sauce and sugar. Then mix in the sweet potato flour and the chopped onions and water chestnuts. Leave to marinate in a refrigerator for about two hours.

Cut up the beancurd skin into strips of 14 cm width. Then cut each strip into equal lengths of 15 to 20 cm.

Put two strips of lean meat and one strip of fat near the edge along the length of a beancurd skin; leave a gap of about 2 cm on either side. Sprinkle some of the chopped onions and water chestnuts over the meat. Use a finger or brush to spread the starchy paste from the Lor Bak marinate on the length of the beancurd skin away from you to act as a seal. Wrap the skin tightly over the Lor Bak filling. Twist the beancurd skin at both ends. Set aside and make more Lor Bak with the remaining skins and filling.

Use a fork to pierce a few holes along each Lor Bak to allow the steam to escape when deep-fried.

Heat up the oil for deep frying in a frying pan. The oil should not be too hot, otherwise the beancurd will be burnt and the meat remain uncooked. Fry 4 or 5 rolls together in the pan. Remove when the Lor Bak turns light brown. Drain and place on kitchen tissue to absorb the excess oil.

Cut into bite-size pieces and serve with Heh Chnee (page 95), sliced cucumber, the *lor* and chilli sauce. You can also serve with fried tau kwa and hard-boiled eggs.

Lor

Warm up – not boil – the stock and stir in the cornflour or tapioca flour slowly to thicken the stock. Add the five-spice powder, sugar and light soya sauce. Bring to the boil, stirring continuously until the cloudy mixture turns brown and transparent. Simmer for a minute.

Beat the egg white slightly to break it up but not till foamy. Pour the egg white into the sauce and stir slowly (not too long) to form long white streaks of egg white in the *lor*. Too much stirring will break the egg white into streaks that are too short. Serve cold with Lor Bak and Heh Chnee.

Chilli Sauce

Use commercially bottled sweet chilli sauce, slightly diluted with hot water. Add toasted sesame seeds and ground peanut brittle (thor tau thng).

Heh Chnee
(Makes 8)

250 g prawns
½ tsp salt
50 g flour
20 g rice flour
20 g tapioca flour
150 ml water
1/8 tsp kapur (slaked lime) or bicarbonate of soda
1 tsp oil for batter
Oil for deep-frying

Heh Chnee or prawn fritter is always served with Lor Bak. The smaller white prawns are preferable for making Heh Chnee because the prawns are fried in the batter with the shells intact and only the heads removed. Bigger prawns, especially the black variety, have thicker and tougher skins. The best prawn fritters are crispy and do not have too much batter. You want to taste the prawns and not the batter.

There are other types of prawn fritters in Penang. Those in Chneh Hu are thin and crispy, and you can hardly see the prawns in it. The prawn fritters in the *mamak* Pasembor or Indian Rojak have more batter.

Wash the prawns, remove the heads and marinate the prawns with the salt.

Sieve the flour, rice flour and tapioca flour together into a container and gradually add the water, stirring continuously to obtain a consistent texture. It is difficult to get rid of the lumps if water is added too quickly. Mix in the kapur and oil. The batter should be quite liquid. Finally, put in the prawns and mix well. Heat up the frying pan, then pour in enough oil to fill the pan to 1 cm. Heat up the oil. Drop a drop of the batter into the oil. If it sizzles the oil is ready for frying.

Spread 4 or 5 prawns without overlapping them and some batter on the pan; spread them in a circle about 7 - 8 cm. There should be a thin batter between the prawns. Add more batter to fill any gaps between the prawns and to form a neat circle. If the batter covering the prawns is too thick, add a bit of water to the batter to thin it out. Fry both sides till golden brown. Drain and place on kitchen tissues to absorb the excess oil. Repeat with the remaining prawns and batter.

Serve with Lor Bak, cucumber slices, chilli sauce and *lor*.

BAK MOI
RICE PORRIDGE

Bak Moi is pork rice porridge and the main ingredient, *bak,* in Hokkien, is 'meat', in this case, pork; *moi* is 'rice porridge'. You can use minced and/or sliced pork as well as other parts of the animal like the liver, the kidney and the brains. An egg can be added if you wish.

The two Bak Moi stalls we frequent are the ones at the Kampong Malabar and Penang Road junction, and at the junction of Lorong Selamat and Macalister Road. At the latter, you have a choice of *moi* or *chok.* Hokkien *moi* is grainy rice porridge while Cantonese *chok* is more gluey as it has been cooked till the rice grains have disintegrated. You could have noodles instead – bee hoon, rice vermicelli or mee suah, a Hokkien wheat flour vermicelli.

When I was young, I lived in my grandmother's house in Macalister Road, diagonally opposite the junction with Lorong Selamat, so I am an old-time customer of the Bak Moi stall. When I moved away from the area, I still returned to eat at the stall or take away the Bak Moi. In the days before plastic bags, the Bak Moi was packed in ceramic jars covered with brown paper and tied with the traditional *kiam chau* to provide a handle for carrying the porridge home.

Kiam chau is a string that is made from grass. Hence, its name in Hokkien literally means 'salty grass'. It was widely used before we had raffia and other man-made strings. Some Bak Chang in Penang are still tied with *kiam chau.* Younger readers may be wondering where the ceramic jars came from. They were jars in which tong chai (preserved Tianjin cabbage) were sold in. Although a small amount of tong chai is used to flavour a bowl of Bak Moi, it is an important ingredient, so the hawker went through many jars of *tong chai* a day. Such use of the jar is an early example of recycling. If you returned the jar for your next take-away you would get a discount.

A good pork or chicken stock is important for cooking Bak Moi. Like many other porridges, rice porridge thickens or coagulates when it cools down. It will do the same even if water is added and the porridge is boiled again. Hence the Bak Moi should be eaten hot.

Spring onions are used to flavour the minced meat, boiled in the porridge and used as a garnish. Fried chopped garlic gives Bak Moi an extra zing. Eu Char Kuih or Chinese cruellers, bought from the market, are a traditional accompaniment to Bak Moi.

Recyclable tong chai *jar used for taking away rice porridge.*

Bak Moi
(Serves 4)

250 g rice
1.2 litre water

Stock
500 g chicken or pork bones
1 litre water

150 g pork
80 g spring onions
3 tsp tong chai (preserved radish)
1 tbsp corn flour or tapioca flour
3 tbsp light soya sauce
250 g minced lean pork
1 tsp sesame oil
Ground pepper to taste
2 tsp salt
6 eggs (optional)
Eu Char Kuih (Chinese cruellers), cut into 1 cm slices
Fried chopped garlic
4 fresh red chillies, sliced

When Cooking in a Rice Cooker
Wash the rice, drain and cook it in an electric rice cooker with 500 ml of water. When the rice is cooked and the rice cooker switches off automatically, add another 500 ml of water, stir thoroughly and switch on the rice cooker again. The liquid in the rice cooker could overflow if the cooker is covered, therefore cooked uncovered or leave a gap. If the rice cooker switches off automatically again, give the porridge a thorough stir, especially at the bottom of the pot and switch on again. Cook the porridge for a total of about 30 minutes after the first automatic switch off. Add the rest of the water for the porridge, stir thoroughly, and leave the porridge in the rice cooker on the 'keep-warm' mode.

When Cooking in a Saucepan
Wash the rice, drain and cook the rice in a saucepan with the 1.2 litre of water. Turn down the heat to low when the rice comes to a boil and simmer for at least an hour, stirring every 10 minutes.

To make the stock, boil the water with the bones, lower the flame and simmer for at least ½ hour, preferably one hour.

Slice the pork thinly, to about 2 to 3 cm thickness.

Chop a stalk of spring onions finely and set aside as garnish. Cut up the white portion of the remaining spring onions finely and keep aside for making the meatballs. Cut the remaining spring onion leaves into lengths of about 4 cm for cooking in the Bak Moi.

Coarsely chop up the tong chai. Divide it into two equal portions, one for the meatballs and the other for cooking in the Bak Moi.

Mix the tapioca or cornflour, 1 tbsp light soya sauce,

the chopped white section of the spring onions and one portion of the tong chai together. Combine with the minced pork, the sesame oil and the ground pepper. Use a teaspoon to fashion the minced pork mixture into balls of about 2 cm to 3 cm in diameter.

Divide the porridge, sliced meat, meatballs, 4-cm lengths of spring onions, tong chai and chopped spring onion garnish into two equal portions. Boil one portion of the rice porridge with about half the stock (about 400 ml).

Add 1 tbsp of light soya sauce and 1 tsp of salt to the porridge. Drop one portion of the meatballs into the porridge, stirring constantly. Now add the sliced pork with the 4-cm lengths of spring onions and the reserved tong chai. Stir and allow to boil.

If you are using sliced liver and kidney, add them at this stage. Stir again and allow to boil.

Repeat for the remaining portion of porridge and ingredients.

If you wish, break an egg into each portion of the Bak Moi, stirring vigorously to break up the egg.

Garnish the Bak Moi with finely chopped spring onions, sliced Eu Char Kuih and fried chopped garlic. Serve with light soya sauce and sliced red chillies.

Eu Char Kuih, according to Chinese folklore, represents the Song dynasty official Qin Hui and his wife, Lady Wang. They were regarded as traitors who plotted against and caused the death of the patriotic General Yue Fei. The twin pieces of deep fried dough is a symbol of how the couple should have been executed for their evil.

My mother explained how Mee Sua Chien is cooked, but I don't remember ever seeing her prepare this scrumptious dish at home.

MEE SUA CHIEN
CRISPY FRIED MEE SUA
(Serves 8)

Mee sua is a wheat vermicelli which has a smooth, starchy texture when cooked. It is a Chinese longevity noodle, a speciality of Xiamen in Fujan Province. It is the custom among the Nonya community to serve a person mee sua on the morning of his or her birthday.

Traditionally, mee sua was sold in boxes but, more recently, they are packed in plastic bags. The mee sua comes in bunches of various sizes and each bunch is tied together with a thin, red thread. The dry mee sua is quite salty – presumably with salt added to preserve it – and must be soaked in boiled water to soften it before cooking. However, this should be done just before the mee sua is cooked, otherwise it will become too soggy. For the same reason, mee sua soup should be eaten very soon after it is cooked.

Mee Sua Chien is mee sua fried with crab meat, potato starch and egg till the mee sua is dry and crispy. It is garnished with spring onions and fried shallots. I have cooked this dish numerous times and I find that it is extremely important to get the correct proportion of the mee sua and the egg. It doesn't taste quite right if too much mee sua or egg is used. I call it Mee Sua Chien to differentiate it from Mee Sua Char (mee suah fried with some gravy like Hokkien Char) and Mee Sua Tau (mee sua cooked with a thick gravy)

This dish must be fried in individual portions, and this recipe is for four. You should not fry large portions unless you have a large wok and a hot fire. Mee Sua Chien should be eaten piping hot.

200 g mee sua (4 to 6 bunches)
6 shallots
3 cloves garlic
4 stalks spring onions
6 eggs
2 tsp light soya sauce
5 tbsp oil (including 1 tbsp for frying shallots)
8 tsp sweet potato flour
8 tbsp water
¼ tsp salt
7 tsp oil
120 g crab meat

Peel and thinly slice the shallots. Smash the garlic, remove the skin and chop up the garlic finely. Clean and cut the spring onions into 3-4 mm lengths. Divide these prepared ingredients into 8 portions.

Break 6 eggs, beat the egg white first, avoiding the yolks, then break up yolks. The egg should not be beaten up like for omelette where the yolk and whites are mixed well. Add 2 tsp of light soya sauce.

Heat 1 tbsp of the oil in a wok. Fry the sliced shallots till just light brown. Divide into eight equal portions.

Mix 8 tsp of the sweet potato flour with 8 tbsp of water. Add to this ¼ tsp of salt. Boil a kettleful of water for soaking the mee sua.

Soak 50 g (1 to 1½ bunch) of mee sua in a large bowl of boiling water.

Heat ½ tsp of oil in a wok. When the oil is hot, put in a quarter of the chopped garlic and fry till nearly brown. Add a quarter of the crab meat and stir briefly and spread the crab meat uniformly in a circle in the wok

Untangle the soften mee sua in the boiling water so that it is not bunched together. Pick up the mee sua

from the water with chopsticks and spread it evenly over the crab. Do not stir the mixture.

Stir the sweet potato mixture and drizzle about 2 tbsp of it evenly over the mee sua, especially around the edge of the circle. Similarly, spread ¼ of the beaten egg on the mee sua. Now, put a portion of the sliced spring onions and a portion of the partially fried shallot over the egg.

Use the frying ladle to separate the fried mee sua from the wok to check if the mee sua has browned. If so, flip the mee sua over with the frying ladle. Drizzle ½ tsp of oil around the edge of the mee sua and fry till the egg side of the Mee Sua Chien is cooked

Spread another portion each of the fried shallots and sliced spring onions over the Mee Sua Chien. Turn it over and cut it into quarters with the frying ladle. Repeat for remaning ingredients.

The Mee Sua Chien should be served hot with Suan Yong Chor (see page 64) or chilli sauce.

HU PEOW THNG
FISH MAW SOUP
(Serves 16)

Hu Peow Thng is a Nonya soup which is normally served for anniversary occasions like birthdays (of the living and the departed), Chinese New Year and *cheng beng* (Chinese's All Soul's Day).

Hu peow is Hokkien for fish maw or the air bladder which allows the fish to adjust its buoyancy at different depths in the water. As an ingredient, fish maw is dried and deep-fried to make it puff up. By itself it is tasteless; in this soup it soaks up the stock and the flavour of the prawn and pork balls.

Hu peow is a Chinese delicacy and can be very expensive depending on the fish from which it is obtained. Hence, fish maw comes in different sizes and shapes. Some fish maws have medicinal value. That is why they are sold in Chinese medical halls.

Sea cucumber is also reputed to have medicinal properties. In Hokkien it is known as hai som or sea ginseng. Recent research has shown that it is a rich source of chondroitin sulphate. Like glucosamine sulphate, it is known to alleviate arthritis pains.

This is a soup of Hokkien origins using seafood, meat and vegetables like cabbage and carrots. Bangkwang is a later local addition. It is called Hee Peow Thng in Singapore; the variation is due to the difference between the Hokkien dialect spoken in Singapore and Penang. It is served with fried chopped garlic and fried sliced shallots – garnishes which give the soup that oomph!

The secret to a good soup is a good bone stock which should be prepared first.

50 g hu peow (dried fish maw)
30 g dried Chinese mushrooms
3 stalks spring onions
100 g hai som (sea cucumber)
400 g bangkwang (yambean)
300 g cabbage
100 g carrots
1 kg pork bones
3 litre stock from pork bones
2 tbsp light soya sauce
1½ tsp salt or to taste
200 g fish balls
1 sprig coriander leaves
2 tbsp oil
4 cloves garlic

Meatballs
250 g minced pork
250 g prawns
2 cloves garlic
1 tbsp cornflour or tapioca flour
¼ tsp ground pepper
½ tsp salt
1 tsp sesame oil
2 tbsp light soya sauce

2 tbsp fried sliced shallots

Soup

To prepare the stock, add the bones to the cold water in a pot and bring to boil. Turn down the heat and let it simmer for at least three hours.

It is more convenient to buy the pre-conditioned sea cucumber. If these are not available the dried sea cucumbers have to be soaked in water for at least 12 hours. They are then cooked over low heat for at least 1 hour.

Cut the sea cucumbers into lengths of about 3cm. Soak the mushrooms in warm water for at least 20 minutes. Remove the stem and cut the caps into into half or quarters. Rinse the spring onions and cut into lengths of about 4 cm.

Skin the bangkwang. Cut the bangkwang into two, then into thin slices of about 2 mm thick. Finally, cut the bangkwang into squares of about 3 cm by 3 cm.

Peel the cabbage into individual leaves. Cut the spines from the leaves and reserve the spines for the soup stock. Stack the leaves together and slice into 3 cm squares.

Rinse and skin the carrots. Cut four v-shaped grooves down the length of the carrots. Slice the carrots into pieces of about 2 to 3 mm thickness.

Smash up the 6 cloves of garlic, remove the skin and chop the garlic finely. Two thirds will be for frying and the other third, for the meatballs.

Meat balls

Shell and de-vein the prawns. Chop them up coarsely.

Mix the minced garlic, cornflour, ground pepper, salt, sesame oil and the light soya sauce with the minced pork and the chopped prawns.

Heat 2 tbsp of oil in a saucepan and fry the minced garlic. Stir continuously to ensure that the garlic is not burnt. Remove most of the garlic from the pan when browned, with a bit of the oil. Set aside.

Add the carrots and the bangkwang and fry for another a minute or so.

Add the stock and bring to the boil. Put in the light soya sauce, cabbage, fish maw, sea cucumber and salt. Bring to a boil again, then simmer for 20 minutes.

Form the meat mixture into balls of about 2 to 3 cm in diameter using two dessert spoons. Drop each ball into the boiling soup. Finally, add the fish balls.

Serve with fried chopped garlic and fried sliced shallots.

LENG CHEE KANG & SEE KO THNG
HERBAL DESSERTS

Leng Chee Kang and See Ko Thng are two related desserts which contain Chinese herbs with nutritional and medicinal values. There is a fine line between food and medicine in Chinese culture, hence many of the herbs are traditionally sold in Chinese medical halls.

Leng Chee Kang is the seed from the lotus plant; it is served with dried logan in syrup.

'Four fruit soup' is the literal translation of See Ko Thng. Presumably there were only four ingredients in the original recipe: lotus seeds, dried longan, ginko nuts and dried persimmons. We used to eat these desserts at the night-time hawker centre at the Esplanade, one of the early hawker centres in Penang in the days when most hawkers plied the streets. There were certainly many more trays of ingredients in that Esplanade See Ko Thng stall. Besides the four original ingredients, I recall others like pak hup (dried lily bulb), Chinese barley, candied winter melon, getah angul, phong tai hai and agar-agar. White cloud ear fungus (*Tremella juciformis*) which comes from Fujian province is another ingredient for See Ko Thng. Getah angul is a gum from a tree and phong tai hai is a dried fruit which looks like a small Chinese olive (kanna). When soaked in water both expand and have the same texture; only differing in the colour. The getah angul in syrup looks a poor man's bird nest because of their similar texture.

Dried logan used to be sold with the shells and seeds. We had to break the shells and carefully remove the dried dark brown fresh from the seeds. We do not have to go through this process with dried logan flesh available today.

There is a similar dessert in Singapore called Cheng Thng. Both Penang and Singapore versions now have cheaper ingredients like sago pellets to replace some of the more expensive original herbal ingredients and to add bulk to the dessert. It would be more convenient if you bought lotus seeds split into halves and gingko nuts with the bitter cores removed, otherwise you would have to do that yourself. Removing the core from the gingko nut is a bit more challenging! These herbs can still be bought in Chinese medicinal halls and many supermarkets in Malaysia and Singapore today.

See Ko Thng was traditionally served hot but today it is also served cold with ice shavings. More sugar is required if served with ice.

Getah angul and phong tai hai (front).

Leng Chee Kang & See Ko Thng

(Serves 8)

50 g dried logan flesh (long yan rou)
60 g dried lotus seeds (lian zi)
60 g ginko nut (bai guo)
30 g Solomon's seal (yu shu)
30 g Chinese barley (yi mi)
30 g lily bulb (bai he)
30 g agar-agar strips
4 phong tai hai (pang da hai)
10 g getah angul (emas manngor)
40 g sugared winter melon (tang dong gua)
1 dried persimmons (shi bing)
30 g white cloud ear fungus (bai mu er)
220 g rock sugar
5 *Pandanus* leaves
1.5 litre water for syrup

Soak the dried longan in water for about ½ hour. Split the dried lotus seeds into two and check that the green shoots have been removed. Soak the lotus seeds in water for about 2 hours.

Crack the ginko nut shell and extract the nut. Boil for 2 minutes and remove the brown skin. To remove the core, which is bitter, push a toothpick from the base of each nut through to the other side. Soak the gingko nuts in water for about 2 hours.

Cut the agar-agar into strips of about 3 cm and soak them in water for about 2 hours. Similarly, soak the barley, the dried lily petals, white fungus and Solomon's seal in water for about 2 hours. The barley should be soaked separately because it has to be cooked first. Cut the Solomon's seal into shorter strips and break up the white fungus into smaller pieces.

Soak the phong tai hai in water for about 2 hours. When it has fully expanded, remove and discard

Leng Chee Kang – lotus seeds served with dried longan in syrup.

the thin dark brown outer skin and the brown veins. Carefully remove the transparent brown phong tai hai which tends to be linked together in one long piece, and leave behind the sediment. Pick up the phong tai hai, rinse with cold water and set aside.

Soak the getah angul in water for at least 2 hours. Remove the brown sediment and carefully remove the transparent getah angul from the water. Rinse the getah angul in cold water and set aside.

Cut the winter melon into strips. Rinse the white powder off the dried persimmon and cut the persimmon into thin slices.

Ideally, the barley, lotus seeds, gingko nuts, the lily bulbs and the Solomon's seal should all be boiled separately since they take different times to cook. Barley takes longest to cook, next the lotus seeds and then the gingko nuts.

It is more convenient to cook the ingredients in one pot, so the ingredient that takes longest to cook should be boiled first, followed by others which cook faster.

Place the barley in about a litre of water in a pot and bring to the boil. Then add the lotus seeds and the gingko nuts. Simmer for about 5 minutes.

Add the Solomon's seal, bring to boil then simmer for another 10 minutes. Include the lily bulb petals, bring to boil then simmer for another 10 minutes. Finally, put in the white fungus, bring to boil then simmer for another 5 minutes. Drain the water and rinse the ingredients in cold water.

To prepare the syrup, boil the 1.5 litres of water with the rock sugar and the *pandanus* leaves. When the sugar has dissolved, add the boiled ingredients, the diced winter melon, the sliced persimmon and the dried logan and simmer for about 5 minutes.

Finally, add the agar-agar, getah angul and the phong tai hai. The dessert is ready for serving hot or cold.

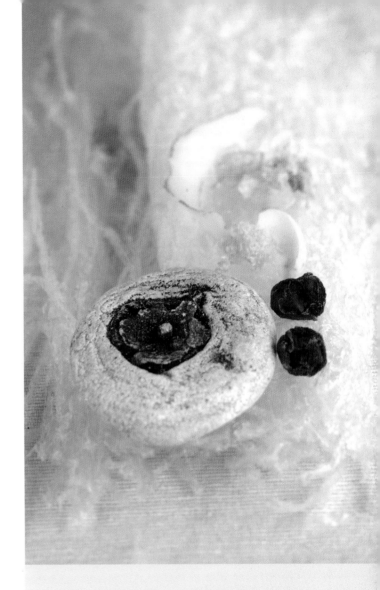

(Anti-clockwise from front): Dried persimmon, dried longan flesh, lily bud petal, white cloud ear fungus and Solomon's seal. These items are placed on agar agar strips.

HUAN CHOO THNG
SWEET POTATO SOUP

(Serves 6)

300 g sweet potatoes
5 cm old ginger
30 g demerara sugar (brown sugar)
600 ml water

Huan Choo Thng is Hokkien for sweet potato soup. It is a simple traditional dessert of diced sweet potato boiled with old ginger and demerara sugar (brown, unrefined sugar). The ginger gives the plain sweet potato a distinctive fragrance and a slightly spicy-hot taste. Ginger is believed to help digestion and to alleviate nausea. The good thing about the demerara sugar is that it free from harmful chemicals and preservatives and retains all the natural vitamins and minerals present in cane sugar.

Sweet potatoes come in various sizes and different skin and flesh colours, from yellow, cream, orange to maroon. To prevent having different cooking times for different types of potatoes, it is best to choose one type of sweet potato each time you cook this dish.

Skin the sweet potatoes and cut into 2.5 cm cubes. Keep them submerged in water to prevent them from discolouring. Clean the ginger and cut into slices of about 3 mm thickness.

Bring the water with the sliced ginger to a boil. Lower the flame and simmer for about 10 minutes. Add the sweet potatoes and bring to the boil again before simmering for another 10 minutes.

Finally, include the sugar. Use a fork to pierce the potato to check if it is soft; if not, simmer until done. Some potatoes take longer to cook than others. The sweet potato pieces will break up if over-cooked.

This dessert can be served hot or warm.

HAINANESE INFLUENCE

IT IS DIFFICULT TO GET THE PENANG HAINANESE FOOD that I grew up with today. Many of the dishes served now have mutated to such an extent that they have lost their original tastes. I am referring to dishes like Min Chee and Roti Babi. These dishes used to be served at the Garden Hotel and Hollywood Restaurant at Tanjong Bungah. Some of them were also served at Chooi Lim Koo at Ayer Itam and Loke Thye Kee at the junction of Burmah Road and Penang Road. Although there are similarities to Hainanese food in Singapore and Kuala Lumpur, the Penang variety has some distinct characteristics due to the strong Penang Nonya influence.

The Hainanese were the last Chinese immigrants to arrive in Penang and other parts of Malaya. Arriving in the 1920s after the other dialect groups had established their control over most trades and industries, it was difficult for Hainanese men to be employed in better jobs. So they ended up as cooks and domestic helpers to the colonial British.

This was possible, because, by tradition in Hainan Island, it was the men who stayed at home – and did the cooking – while the women toiled in the fields. So, a large number of Hainanese men became cooks and houseboys in British homes and establishments like military messes, recreation clubs and canteens. The then Georgetown Municipal Council (later the City Council) had in their building at the Esplanade a canteen that served good Hainanese food. Some of the clubs, like the Penang Sports Club and the Penang Swimming Club, still have the remnants of this traditional food and culture. Even the restaurant in the non-British Chinese Swimming Club was run by Hainanese, first Ah Sin from 1928 to 1948, then Ah Cheng. Ah Sin's family still runs Zealand Cafe in Gurney Drive.

Most of the holiday bungalows and guest houses in the then Malayan hill stations of Penang Hill, Maxwell Hill, Fraser's Hill and Cameron Highlands were exclusively taken care of by Hainanese families. They also managed and cooked at Rest Houses – Government-run hotels used by civil servants when they travelled around Malaya on duty.

I can remember the good times and good food my extended family had in the holiday bungalows on Penang Hill. Although my aunties and grandmother brought food from home, we enjoyed the fabulous meals prepared by the Hainanese cook cum caretaker. We were well fed for breakfast, lunch, tea and dinner. Cakes and curry puffs fresh out of

Dinner of old family friends at Garden Hotel in Tanjong Bungah. The Chicken Pie has obviously just been served.

On our way to the holiday bungalow on Penang Hill.
My mother is on the extreme left and my grandmother is in the trishaw.
I am in the back row on the right.

the oven tasted heavenly! My mother learned to make puff pastry and perhaps chicken pie from one of the cooks.

The Hainanese had on-the-job training from their British employers. They not only learned to prepare British dishes but also very successfully introduced local ingredients and spices into many of them. So, we have dishes like Min Chee, curry puff, pork chop, chicken stew, chicken pie and mutton stew. Hainanese Pork Chop is certainly more appetizing than the plain chops with boiled vegetables and gravy.

The Hainanese also learned the English language and English etiquette from their employers. This would later come in very useful when they worked in or ran their own cafes and restaurants which catered to British expatriates. Virtually all the colonial food and beverage establishments in Penang (like E&O Hotel) and the rest of Malaya were once served by the Hainanese. Indeed, there is a captain in the Coliseum Café in Kuala Lumpur who has worked there all his life.

Many of the Hainanese moved on to run *kopi tiam* (coffee shops), cafes, restaurants and bakeries. At one time, the Hainaneses owned about ninety percent of the *kopi tiam* in Penang but, today, the percentage is significantly less.

In the 1950s or earlier, there was a well-known Hainanese *kopi tiam* at the junction of Dicken Street and Penang Road, next to what was the Cathay Cinema, or Queen's Theatre to my parents' generation. My family still refers to this popular eating place as being 'next to Queen's' even though the theatre no-longer exists. The site is now occupied by a shop called Mydin. The coffee shop was unique because it had two storeys. There was a wide flight of steps from the front of the shop leading to the upper level. The lower or street level was at Dicken Street at the back of the shop where drinks and food were prepared. There was also a fairly large area in front of the *kopi tiam* where several hawker stalls congregated, serving Hainanese Satay, Koay Teow Thng, Ark Thui Mee Sua, Loh Bak and Mamak Poh Piah, among many other Penang heritage dishes. We could eat in the open under the shade of the sea almond trees or inside the coffee shop if it rained.

The kopi tiam *"next to Queens", circa 1930s, on the extreme left.
In the 1950s, hawkers which clustered in front of the coffee shop, sold a variety
of Penang favourites, including Loh Bak and Mamak Poh Piah.*

Tip Top, a Hainanese cafe at Pulau Tikus, was well-known in its time for curry puffs, cream puff and cakes. These were taken away in nice cardboard boxes which were uncommon in those days. The puff pastry used for the curry puffs must have been learned from the British while the filling was probably influenced by the Indian Samosa. Several cafes in Penang served Western Hainanese food as well as cakes and pastries. Wing Lok and Kuan Lok, both housed in buildings owned by Khoo Sian Ewe, a very prominent member of the Penang Straits Chinese community and one of the largest private land owners in Penang before the Second World War, were such bar and cafe establishments.

For a long time, I wondered why the Hainanese also cooked Nonya food. Then I remembered what my mother told me – that when she was young, her father, Khoo Beng Chiang†, employed a Hainanese *cham phor* or cook. So, it was common for the wealthy Nonya families who wanted to enjoy both 'English' as well as Nonya food at home to employ Hainanese cooks.

This explains why the Hainanese came to master Nonya food like Gulai Tumis, Curry Kapitan, serve Sambal Belacan with their fried noodles, and Sambal Pencuri with their stewed mutton. This Nonya influence represents a second strand of Penang Hainanese heritage food. The Hainanese also modified some Nonya dishes like Roti Babi and Choon Piah to suit the Western taste.

† I did not know my grandfather because he passed away early on. I had often heard my mother mention his company, Keat Chiang, which I understand was in New Bridge Road in Singapore. I found out from one of my elder cousins, Khoo Teng Lam, who was very close to him, that grandfather was a millionaire and a philanthropist. He was the founding Deputy Chairman of United Chinese Bank, which is now part of UOB in Singapore, and was also the founder of Penang's Chung Ling High School. He was from China but my grandmother, Tan Siew Kee, was from a typical Nonya family in Balik Pulau.

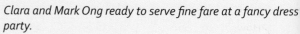

Clara and Mark Ong ready to serve fine fare at a fancy dress party.

The E&O Hotel on it's seafront site has been patronised by colonial administrators, planters and the elite of Penang since 1885.

The Coliseum in colonial days was the place where starched-shirt administrators partook of Western food. Today, it's patronised by those who hanker for colonial atmosphere.

The Hainanese and Nonya influences in the food of Khoo Sian Ewe's family is reflected in the book, *Penang Palate*, written by his grand-daughter, Yeap Joo Kim. Two Hainanese brothers who used to cook for the Khoos founded Loke Thye Kee, the well-known restaurant that served both Hainanese versions of Western and Nonya food. In fact, Khoo Sian Ewe helped the brothers set up the restaurant in the building that belonged to him.

Loke Thye Kee (see page 3), founded in 1919 and built like a ship, claims to be the oldest restaurant in Penang. It was reputedly a popular venue for young couples and matchmaking‡. There was an inconspicuous entrance on the ground floor with food served on the deck-like first and second floors. Alfreso dining was already the in thing in Penang in the early 20th century! The restaurant closed many years ago but I have it on good authority that Loke Thye Kee will be revivied.

Just as Loke Thye Kee added spice to Penang's social life, Worcestershire sauce, made famous by the Lea & Perrins brand, is important to giving flavour to Penang Hainanese food – in fact as important as cheow cheng (light soya bean sauce) is to Hokkien food. The Hainanese and the Nonyas made their own Worcestershire sauce. My mother and my Aunty Nooi made their own versions too.

Hainanese Satay Babi is a very unique Penang dish, although it is not very commonly found, even in Penang, today. It is yet another example of fusion food of that era. The satay sauce is not peanut-based but is made of sweet potato and not so spicy. Today, the best Satay Babi is from a stall that is parked in Bangkok Lane on certain days of the week. It used to move around the Pulau Tikus area on Tuesdays and Thursdays. There was a very popular stall at the Hainanese *kopi tiam* next to Queen's.

Interestingly, Hainanese Chicken Rice in Penang does not have the high profile that it has in Singapore, Malacca or Kuala Lumpur. I suspect that Hainanese Chicken Rice has fused with the Cantonese Pak Cham Kai popular in Penang. Hainanese Chicken Rice is cooked with ginger, garlic and chicken stock, while the Cantonese chicken is served red-at-the-bone with plain rice.

It is still possible to find a few places that serve some Hainanese food in Penang. However they do not serve the wide range of food that was served at Hollywood restaurant or Garden Hotel. Another restaurant that served both Western and Nonya Hainanese food was Ilham next to the Penang Sports Club, right at the Western Road end of Macalister Road. At one time, we could get chicken pies at one of the restaurants at the Penang Swimming Club – so long as you made your order one day in advance.

A better restaurant today is at Chulia Lane. It is incredibly busy especially during long holiday weekends. They still serve mainly Nonya food including an authentic Gulai Tumis cooked with Tow Theh, a larger species of White Pomfret. However, the price for this dish is high by Penang standard. You could even order fried tanau kiamhu (salt fish) to go with it. There is also an old eating shop in China Street which serves Nonya food as well as chicken and pork chops. It is not so classy and not the same as the ones we used to get, but you can get a credible Roti Babi there.

‡ *From what I have heard from my Auntie Nell in Singapore, there is a Hainanese restaurant in Singapore – Mooi Chin – that hosted the same social function.*

CURRY PUFF

Curry puffs probably evolved from the Indian Samosa (see page 164). In Penang, there are various types of curry puffs, ranging from this version – made from puff pastry, the early Kali Pok, and the more common and familiar deep-fried curry puff.

The curry puff produced by this recipe was traditionally made by the Hainanese who cooked for the British in pre-independence Malaya. Puff pastry, so different from the pastries of the Malay and Nonya versions of this snack, indicates the British connection. The filling, which could have been influenced by that of the samosa, is made up of minced mutton, onions and a little potato – unlike today's store-bought curry puffs which have more potatoes than onions. Chicken can be used, but I find that if I substitute lamb or mutton with chicken fillet, the filling tastes a bit *siap*, a Hokkien word to describe a dry, sappy taste. That is because there is less fat in chicken fillet. More potatoes should be added to counter the effect. The curry puff is glazed with beaten egg and baked.

We used to buy curry puffs from Tip-Top, a café in Pulau Tikus, and Wing Lok Café in Penang Road. Both cafés also served cream puffs, cream horns, Swiss rolls and various Western cakes. The cakes did not use real cream, only butter cream. When we stayed in the bungalow on Penang Hill, we were served hot curry puffs and cakes for tea by the Hainanese caretaker cum cook.

I have not used my mother's recipe for the puff pastry, instead I suggest using commercially available frozen pastry. It is best to choose a well-known brand; they seem to puff up more. For the uninitiated, you would need some practice rolling the pastry. You do not need a rolling pin; I have used an old wine bottle in my student days. There is another option in ready-rolled pastry.

Kali Pok is a Malayan Hokkien transliteration of curry puff. The version that we ate when I was young had a basic pastry enclosing a spiced potato-based filling with a touch of minced meat, if at all. The pastry was folded into an irregular triangular/semi-elliptical shape and deep-fried. I remember the Chinese hawker that went around on his tricycle with a large box in front. The box contained a small charcoal fire around which he arranged his Kali Pok to keep them warm.

Today, the commonly available deep-fried curry puffs are the semi-elliptical ones made by the Nonyas and the Malays in Malaysia, Singapore and Thailand. Traditionally, the Malay version is sometimes known as Epok-Epok but, in more recent times, they have been called Kari Pap – a Malay transliteration of curry puff. Various types of pastries are employed and the filling is traditionally mainly spiced mashed potatoes and minced meat, usually chicken. The cheaper versions have less meat or none at all. Malays also used tinned sardines as a filling. The Chinese, especially in Singapore, has recently incorporated hardboiled eggs into the fillings of the curry puffs. The Malay Epok-Epok pastry is basic while the Nonya pastry mixes two types to get the spiral puff after deep-frying.

Curry Puff

(Makes 32)

Filling

250 g minced mutton or lamb
100 g potatoes
300 g onions
2 tbsp curry powder for meat
1 tbsp oil
½ tsp salt
1 tbsp coconut milk or dairy milk
1 sprig curry leaves

Puff Pastry

2 packets puff pastry (375 g each)
Plain flour for dusting pastry and the worktop
1 egg, beaten

Filling

Peel and dice potatoes into ½ cm cubes. Peel and wedge onions, then cross-wise into about 7 x 7 mm. Mix the curry powder with 4 tbsp water to form a liquid paste.

Put the oil in a hot frying pan or wok. Fry the potatoes till they are nearly transparent and soft, then mash them coarsely in the wok. Put aside.

Add more oil if needed and fry the onions till transparent. Include the curry paste and stir. Add a little water if the curry paste is too dry and sticks to the pan. When fragrant, add the minced meat and the salt. As the minced meat tends to be lumpy, use the ladle to break it up.

Return the potatoes to the pan. Add the curry leaves and continue frying. Include the milk or coconut milk and fry for a minute. Remove.

Puff Pastry

Thaw the puff pastry, if it is frozen, by transferring it from the freezer to the refrigerator.

Clear a clean and smooth work-top or use a pastry board. Spread a small amount of flour uniformly over the surface and over the puff pastry. Apply pressure on the rolling pin evenly over the width of the pastry. The pastry will become thinner and wider. Try to keep the shape of the pastry rectangular. Sprinkle a small amount of flour on the work surface and spread flour on the pastry to keep the pastry from sticking. Repeat for the length of the pastry. The pastry will continue to become thinner and broader. Try to keep the shape of the pastry rectangular. Sprinkle flour on the work surface and pastry.

Repeat these steps until the pastry is about 2 to 3 mm thick and the pastry is approximately 32 x 40 cm. Trim the sides of the rolled pastry to make it rectangular. Keep the strips aside and roll them again to maximize the use of pastry.

Cut the pastry lengthwise into four strips and width-wise also into four strips, giving 16 pieces of pastry each about 10 x 8 cm. Take each piece of the pastry and increase the length a little by rolling the pin along the middle section, avoiding the ends. These edges will puff up when baked.

Use a pastry brush to coat near the edges of half of each piece of pastry with beaten egg, taking care not to coat the very edge of the pastry as this will prevent the pastry from puffing up. Spread the filling on one half of the pastry, keeping about 1 cm of the edge free. Fold the pastry over and gently press the three open edges together.

Preheat the oven to 240°C. Place the curry puffs on a baking tray and bake for about 15 minutes till the pastry is golden brown. Cool and serve.

MIN CHEE

Min Chee or Bin Chee is a Hainanese dish made up of diced potatoes, carrots, chicken, mushrooms, onions and green peas. It is accompanied by mashed potatoes and fried eggs together with croutons and fried sliced shallots as garnish. This popular dish, a meal in itself, was on the menus of the Hollywood Restaurant and the Garden Hotel at Tanjong Bungah when I was young. It was served with Worcestershire sauce or ang mor tau eu – white man's soya sauce in Penang Hokkien. My mother cooked a version at home without the carrots, peas, mashed potatoes and egg, and occasionally with the croutons and fried sliced shallot.

There are two possible origins of Min Chee. It could be a Hainanese version of the English mixed vegetables, which consist of boiled carrots, peas, beans and suede. The Hainanese chefs added diced chicken, potatoes, and tinned mushrooms to make it a more complete dish. The tinned button mushrooms have a slightly denser texture than fresh mushrooms which were not available in colonial Malaya. Influenced by the Nonya practise of cutting ingredients finely, the potatoes and carrots were diced into small cubes. Whole cloves, cinnamon bark and soya sauce were added to give Min Chee its subtle flavour. The Min Chee was placed in a serving plate surrounded by piped mash potatoes and topped with fried eggs and garnished with fried sliced shallots and croutons.

Min Chee would not be Min Chee if it is not accompanied by the very quintessential English condiment – Worcestershire sauce. Lea and Perrins is the brand that we in Malaysia and Singapore are more familiar with although the Hainanese cooks and many Nonya families have their own recipes.

In the old days, we added Worcestershire sauce to our own portion of Min Chee. The Min Chee that is served in one Penang restaurant has Worcestershire sauce added in the cooking. It is rather sad that the cooks of this generation do not know the original taste of Min Chee and the new generation of Penangites associate this mutation as the true Min Chee.

Another possible origin for Min Chee is that it is a corruption of 'mince' as in minced lamb or beef; the recipe being derived from Shepherd's Pie, which uses lamb, or Cottage Pie, which uses beef, carrots and onions.

There is a version of this dish in Singapore which uses minced pork or beef but does not include carrots or mushrooms, adding credence that Min Chee could have evolved from Shepherd's or Cottage Pie.

I have also found a Macau version also called Minchee which is claimed as a Mecanese national dish. The ingredients are ground pork or beef, onions, fried potatoes and soya sauce.

Aunty Jane from my wife's side of the family cooks a similar dish to fill the Pai Ti shells. I found the dish called Kroket Tjanker (Java Kwei Patti) in Susie Hing's *In a Malayan Kitchen*. It must have originated from Indonesia with nominal Dutch influence. There are similarities between the fillings for the *kroket* (or *croquette* in French and English) and the Java Kwei Patti. The main ingredients are minced or finely diced cooked meat cooked with diced mushroom and thicken with a white sauce.

My family in London has a variation on this dish influenced by Shepherd's and Cottage Pie. We cover the Min Chee with mashed potato and bake or grill it, sometimes adding grated cheese. This evolution of Min Chee has indeed gone through a full circle from its English origins to the Penang Hainanese variation and back to Britain – a true fusion food! Our version is very popular among our English friends.

Min Chee
(Serves 12)

200 g potatoes
200 g carrots
200 g button mushrooms, tinned or fresh
500 g chicken, deboned
200 g onions
200 g peas
2 tbsp soya sauce
½ tsp ground pepper
2 tsp salt
3 cm cinnamon bark
5 cloves
6 tsp oil
300 ml water

Garnish
600 g potatoes
40 g butter
Salt to taste
6 eggs
Fried sliced shallot
3 slices bread for crouton
6 tbsp oil for shallow frying crouton

Min Chee
Peel the 200 g of potatoes for the Min Chee. Cut the potatoes, carrots, mushrooms and chicken into ½ cm cubes. Cut the onions into ½ cm cubes and break up into squares. Thaw the peas if frozen. Marinate the chicken with the soya sauce, and ground pepper.

When cooking a large portion it is better to first cook the carrots and potatoes separately. Fry the carrots with 2 tsp oil for about 3 minutes and set aside. Fry the potatoes with 2 tsp oil for about 3 minutes and set aside.

Fry a small portion of the onions with 2 tsp oil for about a minute, then add the chicken. Continue cooking for about another 5 minutes till the chicken is cooked. Add the mushrooms, cinnamon and clove, and fry for 5 minutes. Add the cooked carrots and potatoes and the rest of the onions and continue frying for another 5 min.

Add about 300 ml of water and the peas and let the mixture boil and simmer for about 5 minutes. Min Chee should have some gravy. Remove to a serving dish.

Garnish
Clean the potatoes for the mash and boil them in water until they are soft. Use a fork to test whether the potatoes are cooked. They are ready when you can pierce them easily. Peel and mash the potatoes, adding butter and salt according to taste. As an alternative, you may use instant mash potatoes.

Croutons are best made with bread that is not fresh. Cut slices of bread into 1 cm cubes. Heat 6 tbsp of oil in a wok till smoking hot. If the oil is not hot enough, the bread will absorb it. Fry the cubes of bread, stirring continuously. Turn off the fire once they turn golden. As the croutons will continue to cook even after the fire is turned off, be careful that they do not burn. Remove the croutons with a slotted spoon and put them on kitchen tissue to absorb the oil.

Heat up a pan with ½ tsp of oil to fry the eggs one at a time. Break an egg into the pan, turning it over when the egg white becomes opaque. The yolk should not be overcooked. Make the fried sliced shallots.

Serve the Min Chee with the mashed potatoes on the side with toppings of fried eggs, croutons and fried sliced shallots. Offer Worcestershire sauce for diners to season their servings according to taste.

Variation
Transfer the Min Chee to a pie-dish and spread the mashed potato on top. You may also add grated cheese to the topping. Grill at 200°C (400°F) for about 5 minutes until the topping has browned.

HAINANESE CHICKEN STEW

(Serves 12)

This recipe for Hainanese Chicken Stew originated from British kitchens, and the Hainanese cooks introduced local ingredients like soya sauce, cloves and cinnamon to adapt the original chicken stew to suit both the Malayan and the British tastes. The stew uses traditional English ingredients like bacon, boiled eggs, carrots, peas, potatoes and button mushrooms. The gravy is based on a white sauce made of butter, flour and milk.

Hainanese Chicken Stew can be the main course of a Western meal or one of the dishes in a Penang Chinese meal. A simplified version without the peas was a regular feature in our family menu. Worcestershire sauce is an indispensable condiment but it should not be cooked with the stew.

This chicken stew is used as the filling for Hainanese Chicken Pie. For the chicken pie, less water should be used in the recipe.

600 g chicken
1 tsp salt
3 tbsp light soya sauce
½ tsp ground pepper
30 g flour
300 g potatoes
150 g onions
200 g carrots
130 g tinned or fresh button mushrooms
100 g peas
2 small eggs
100 g bacon (optional for stew)
750 ml water (500 ml for pie)
1 stick cinnamon, approx. 3 cm
6 cloves
2½ tbsp oil

Cut the chicken into bite-sized pieces and marinate with the salt, soya sauce and ground pepper. Sprinkle or sieve the flour over the chicken pieces to uniformly coat them.

Peel the potatoes and cut them into 3 cm cubes. Peel and cut onions into four wedges, then cross-wise into eighths. Cut the carrots into 1 x 1 x 2 cm pieces. Cut the mushrooms into two for medium-sized ones or into four for larger mushrooms. If you are using frozen peas, thaw them by soaking them in water.

Put the eggs in a saucepan. Add water to cover the eggs and bring to a boil. Let the eggs boil for a minute, turn off the flame and leave them in hot water for another 5 minutes. Replace the hot water with cold water, then shell the eggs.

Fry the carrots with 1 tablespoonful of oil for about 3 minutes till slightly brown. Drain the oil and set aside the carrots. Fry the potatoes with another spoonful of oil for about 4 minutes till slightly brown. Drain the oil and set the potatoes aside.

Add another tablespoon of oil and fry the chicken pieces. Spread the pieces evenly in the wok. Allow the chicken pieces to cook for 10 minutes until they are browned before turning over. Set the fried chicken aside.

Fry the bacon, if using, in the remaining oil till it is slightly crispy. Cut into pieces of about 3 cm and set aside.

Add more oil if required and fry the onions, separating the layers. Fry till the onions are transparent. Include the chicken, mushrooms, carrots, potatoes, cinnamon stick and cloves. Stir-fry in the wok. Add water and simmer for about 10 to 15 minutes. Include the peas and the boiled eggs towards the end of cooking time.

Arrange the pieces of bacon, if using, on top of the stew and serve with Worcestershire sauce.

Hainanese Chicken Pie has an obvious British origin. No wonder, because the Hainanese were, in colonial times, cooks in British households and establishments.

HAINANESE CHICKEN PIE
(Makes 2)

Hainanese Chicken Pie is a dish we looked forward to during our holidays on Penang Hill.

Use the Hainanese Chicken Stew recipe to make the filling for Hainanese Chicken Pie. However, less water should be used in the stew for the pie filling. In addition, fried bacon is added on top of the filling for a bit of bite and additional flavour.

This pie uses puff pastry which the Hainanese must have learned from the British. They also used the same puff pastry for their well-known curry puffs – the type we used to buy from Tip Top at Pulau Tikus or Wing Lok in town.

I shall not go into the details of making the puff pastry. As with the curry puffs, I suggest using commercial frozen puff pastry. It is best to choose a well-known brand; they seem to puff up more and are crispier. If you want to avoid rolling the pastry, get the rolled pastry.

The conventional way to prepare Hainanese Chicken Pie is to place the pastry over the filling. Make a hole in the pastry to allow the steam from the filling to escape. Do not be greedy and fill the pie dish to the brim; there should be a gap between the filling and the pastry. If the gap is too small, the boiling sauce will wet the pastry, turning it soggy.

I find it better to bake the pastry separately so that it would be crispier while allowing for more filling in the pie. Use the top of the pie dish as the template for cutting the pastry, allowing an extra 2 cm around the perimeter. The pastry can be baked on the cover of the pie dish. When baked, transfer the pastry to cover the pie.

Puff Pastry
1 packet puff pastry (375 g)
1 egg
Plain flour

Pie Filling
Follow the recipe for the chicken stew but use only 500 ml of water. This filling is sufficient for two pies. Place the filling in two pie dishs. Cut 100 g of bacon into 2 cm pieces, fry till slightly crispy and place them on top of the filling.

Puff Pastry
Thaw the puff pastry if it is frozen by transferring it from the freezer to the refrigerator. Divide the pastry into two and roll out the pastry separately. The 375 g of pastry will be sufficient for two pie dishes with diameters or sides less than 20 cm.

Use a clean, smooth worktop or a pastry board; spread a small amount of flour uniformly over the surface. Apply pressure on the rolling pin evenly over the width of the pastry. The pastry will become thinner and wider. Sprinkle a small amount of flour on the work surface and on the pastry.

Roll out the pastry into a rectangle. The longer side should be at least the diameter or length of pie dish plus 12 cm. The width should be at least the diameter or the width of the pie dish plus 12 cm.

Use the pie dish or its cover as a template and cut the pastry allowing 2 cm round the perimeter. Now cut out 3 cm strips around the edge and keep them aside. Transfer the large sheets of pastry on to the cover of the pie dishes or on to a baking tray. Leave the pastry to relax for about 10 minutes.

Beat up the egg. Use a pastry brush to coat a layer of beaten egg on the pastry, taking care not to coat the edge as this would seal it and prevent the pastry from puffing up at the edge when baked. Place the 3 cm strips of pastry cut from the template along the edge of the pastry and brush over with the beaten egg. Roll out the remaining pastry and make shapes to decorate the top of the pies. Brush the pastry, including the decorations, with the beaten egg.

Preheat the oven to 240°C. Bake the pie crusts for about 15 minutes until the pastry is golden brown. The oven temperature can be reduced once the pastry has puffed up. Keep a watchful eye to ensure that they do not burn.

Transfer the baked pastries onto the pie dishes containing the hot filling. Alternatively, bake the crusts of the pies with the filling. In which case, the pie filling should not be hot before baking.

FRIED HAINANESE MEATBALLS
(Serves 4)

This is obviously a variation of an English dish where meat like chicken or pork chop is traditionally served with boiled vegetables and fried potatoes with a gravy.

This, in turn, is a variation of Hainanese Pork Chop, with the chops replaced by fried meatballs. My mother used to cook it regularly. It was very popular with us because of the fried potatoes. The gravy is a typically Hainanese with tomato sauce added to give it a slightly sweet taste. The peas can be replaced by baked beans.

Like Hainanese Pork Chop, this is a complete meal by itself. Although, at home, we serve it as one of several dishes with rice.

As with several other Hainanese dishes, this is traditionally served with Worcestershire sauce on the side.

Meatballs
400 g lean minced pork
120 g onions
50 g carrots
1 egg
2 tbsp flour
1 tbsp light soya sauce
½ tsp salt
Ground pepper
Oil for shallow frying

Garnishes and Sauce
500 g potatoes
220 g onions
200 g carrots
130 g frozen peas
1 tbsp cornflour
1 tbsp light soya sauce
½ tsp salt
¼ cube vegetable or chicken stock
2 tbsp tomato sauce
1 litre water

Peel the onions for the meatballs and chop them up finely, together with the 50 g of carrots.

Peel the potatoes and onions for the garnish. Cut the potatoes into wedges. Slice the onions into rings about 7 mm thick.

Wash the carrots and cut them into 1 x 1 x 2 cm pieces. Thaw the frozen peas by soaking in water. Render 1 tbsp of cornflour in 100 ml of water.

Fry the sliced potatoes in hot oil. Remove the potatoes with a slotted spoon and allow the oil to drain back into the pan. When the potatoes have cooled, heat the oil again and refry them until they are crispy and golden brown.

Meatballs
Thoroughly mix together the minced meat, chopped onions, egg, flour, light soya sauce and salt. Season generously with ground pepper. Divide the mixture into eight portions and compact each portion into a ball. Place on a flat surface and flatten to a thickness of about 2 cm.

Heat a pan. When it is hot, add oil and shallow fry both sides of the patties. For a healthier option, brush each patty with oil and grill under high heat.

Sauce
Heat up a pan. When it is hot, add one teaspoon of oil and saute the carrots for about 2 minutes. Remove the carrots and set aside. Add the onion rings while the pan is still hot. Sauté for about one minute.

Add half of the amount of water, the salt, light soya sauce and the ¼ stock cube and bring to a boil. Put in the rest of the water, the tomato sauce and bring to a boil again.

Add the rendered cornflour, stirring continuously. Turn off the fire when the sauce becomes more transparent.

Put the sauce and the garnishes on a plate and place two patties on top. Serve with Worcestershire sauce.

CURRY KAPITAN

Curry Kapitan is a medium-dry coconut-milk-based chicken curry. It is has the characteristics of a Malay dish which has been adopted by the Penang Nonyas. The spices used are all fresh – chillies, onions, tumeric and lemongrass – plus the most important Belacan (shrimp paste). Curry Kapitan is garnished with a generous serving of eu chang (fried sliced shallot) and fried sliced salt fish (tanau kiam hu).

Legend has it that the dish was prepared by a ship's cook. When asked what was for dinner, the cook replied, "Curry, Kapitan", hence the name. There is a more credible origin for Curry Kapitan. In Ellice Handy's classic *My Favourite Recipes*, there are two recipes called Country Captain. According to the Anglo-Indian Hobson Jobson Dictionary, Country Capitan is the name of a dry curry from Bengal, often served at the table of the skippers of 'country ships', who were themselves called 'country captains'. According to What's Cooking in America (http://whatscookingamerica.net/History/PoultryDishes.htm), this delicious dish, which is known throughout Georgia, dates back to the early 1800s. It is thought that the recipe was brought to Georgia by a British sea captain who had been stationed in Bengal, India and shared it with some friends in the port of Savannah in Georgia.

There could be an Ellice Handy connection here. Ellice Handy was a principal of the Methodist Girl's School in Singapore. Many of the Methodist missionaries were Americans who came to Malaya via India. It is possible that Curry Kapitan could have been brought to Malaya/Singapore via the Southern United States or directly from India by the missionaries.

As for many Malay *gulai* (curries) the ingredients should not be finely ground. You should be able to see small bits of chillies and onions when the curry is cooked.

Traditionally, the Malays use the granite *lesong* (mortar) to pound their *rempah* (spice paste). Therefore the *batu giling* (grinding stone) is not appropriate here.

Curry Kapitan used to be served in Garden Hotel and Hollywood restaurants in Tanjong Bungah. I have not tasted any genuine Curry Kapitan in Penang restaurants recently. Some that I have tried are just like a chicken curry with too many different herbs added.

This is my mother's recipe from one of her cooking demonstrations in the 1950s. From the number of different typed versions, she must have demonstrated this dish on many occasions to the Penang YWCA and the Methodist Girls' School Old Girls' Association.

Some other Curry Kapitan recipes include kaffir leaves and lengkuas. However, following my mother's recipe, I do not believe in including too many herbs and spices and have omit them because I prefer to highlight the individual and distinct flavour of lemongrass.

Curry Kapitan can be served with rice and other dishes or served by itself with some crusty bread. It is accompanied by fried tanau kiam hu.

Tanau Kiam Hu

Curry Kapitan
(Serves 10 with other dishes)

1 medium-sized chicken, about 1.2 kg
1 coconut to give 400 g grated coconut
   or 220 ml concentrated UHT coconut milk
400 ml water
250 g shallots
200 g large onions
120 g fresh chillies
2 stalks lemongrass
4 x 1.5 cm diameter fresh turmeric
6 candlenuts
2 tsp belacan
Salt to taste
1 tsp sugar
10 tbsp coconut oil or other cooking oil

Garnishes
8 shallots, finely sliced and deep-fried
6 x 6 cm tanau kiam hu (fried salt-fish)

Wrap the grated coconut in a muslin cloth and squeeze out about 100 ml of thick coconut milk. Set aside. Now mix the grated coconut with 250 ml of warm water and squeeze out the thin coconut milk. Repeat with a third squeeze after mixing with another 250 ml of warm water. Alternatively, use 220 ml of concentrated pasteurised or UHT coconut milk that is readily available in the shops in Malaysia, Singapore and overseas. Mix 120 ml of the concentrated coconut milk with water to make up 500 ml of the thin coconut milk.

Chop up the chicken into serving pieces; remove the fat and, if preferred, the skin for a healthier alternative.

Slice the belacan thinly and toast till brown. Break up and pound the belacan. Slice the root ends of the lemongrass thinly and pound. Pound the candlenuts.

Slice the turmeric, chillies, onions, shallots and pound together coarsely. Mix all the pounded ingredients together. If a food processor is used, blend the lemongrass and the candlenut first before adding the other ingredients to make a *rempah* (spice paste).

Heat up the oil in a wok or in an earthen pot and fry the *rempah* with the onions till the *rempah* becomes fragrant and turns darker and the onions become transparent. This takes about 15 minutes.

Put the chicken into the fried *rempah* and continue frying for about 5 minutes, gradually adding the thin coconut milk. Simmer for 10 to 15 minutes till the chicken is tender. Add some boiling water if the mixture is too dry. Curry Kapitan is a medium-dry curry, hence the dish should not be too liquid at this stage. Bear in mind that 100 ml of thick coconut milk will be added later. Stir regularly.

Add the thick coconut milk. Bring to the boil and turn off the fire. Add salt to taste.

Sprinkle fried shallots on top of the dish. Serve with rice or bread and fried salt fish.

ROTI BABI

It is most probable that Roti Babi is of Nonya origin. The name of the dish is Malay, and since Malays do not eat pork, it must have originated from the Penang Nonya patois.

This is the version of Roti Babi served in our family. A pocket is cut in a thick slice of bread (*roti*) and a filling is stuffed into it. The filling is traditionally minced pork (*babi*) cooked with onions and yambean (*bangkwang*). The bread is coated with beaten egg and deep-fried.

Roti Babi is served with sliced red chillies and *ang mor tau eu* or Worcestershire sauce. My mother used to make *ang mor tau eu* from an heirloom recipe from the Ong side of the family. My father wrote down the recipe meticulously, counting the number of cumin, fennel and various spices; those were the days before electronic weighing scales, when it was difficult to weigh small quantity of ingredients!

I was told that the Georgetown Municipal (later the City Council) canteen at the Esplanade served good Roti Babi. It is still possible to find Roti Babi in Penang restaurants these days but all too often the dish is soaked in oil. It is definitely not as good as homemade Roti Babi.

In the original Nonya version, the filling is spiced with ground coriander and cekur (a type of ginger) and less vegetables are used. This results in a dry, sappy taste if lean meat is used. This is an example of the subtleties of traditional cooking; there must be a balance between the amount of lean meat and fat, and the proportion of meat and vegetables. I experimented by increasing the amount of lean meat in my Roti Babi on one occasion and my cousin said that it didn't taste right.

Some of the Hainanese cooks who worked for the rich Nonya families in Penang adapted the filling to the Hainanese version. They used cinnamon to give it added flavour.

Some may compare Roti Babi with Roti John, a Malay dish where slices of French loaf are slathered with minced mutton and egg, and fried. To me comparing Roti John to Roti Babi is like comparing chalk and cheese! There is a simplified version of Roti Babi served at the Coliseum in Kuala Lumpur. It is like the fried bread served in English breakfasts but with a meat mixture on the side.

The Italians have something similar – Mozzarella in Carrozza, literally mozzarella in a carriage. As the name implies, mozzarella is the filling used. It is served with an accompaniment of tomato sauce.

For a healthier version of Roti Babi, put the filling between sliced bread and cook in an electric sandwich maker. It would be less oily and doesn't need eggs.

Good old-fashioned bread loaf.

Roti Babi

(Makes 10)

Filling

400 g minced pork or chicken
250 g bangkwang (yambean)*
500 g onions
5 Chinese mushrooms
20 g spring onions
3 cloves garlic
200 g crab meat

Ground pepper
2 tbsp light soya sauce
½ tbsp salt
Water

1 loaf of unsliced bread, preferably at least a day old
6 eggs
50 ml milk
Oil for deep frying
6 fresh red chillies, de-seeded and sliced diagonally
Worcestershire sauce

* If unavailable, carrot or cabbage may be used.

Indian roti (bread) man. (Penang Museum Collection)

Filling

Chop up the yambean into 2 mm cubes. Similarly, chop the onions into 2 mm pieces. You can use a food processor to do the chopping, cutting up the vegetables into smaller pieces before putting them into the food processor. Use the pulse mode and make sure that you do not liquidize the ingredients.

Soak the mushrooms in water. Remove the stalks. Cut the caps into 2 mm cubes. Cut the spring onions into 1 cm lengths. Smash, skin and chop up the garlic finely.

Fry the chopped garlic till it is lightly browned, then add the ground meat. Include the ground pepper, salt and light soya sauce and fry till the meat is cooked. The minced meat tends to stick together in lumps. Use the frying ladle to break it up. If cooking in large quantities, the cooked meat can be broken up using a food processor.

Fry the onions and yambean till the onions are transparent. Stir in the cooked minced pork. Add the crab meat and mix thoroughly in the frying pan. Add a bit of water only if the Roti Babi filling is too dry. The filling should not be so wet that the gravy from the filling will soak into the bread, making it soggy.

Bread

Use a sharp bread knife and slice away the crust at both ends of the bread loaf. Cut the bread into slices of about 2½ to 3 cm thick. Cut away some of the crust on four sides of each slice and bits of the corners also. Do not remove the crust completely or the Roti Babi will be very floppy.

Make a slit in the length of the bread and cut towards the other three sides of the bread to form a pocket. Repeat for all the slices of bread.

Use a small spoon to stuff each slice of bread, pushing the filling towards the edges such that the filling is evenly spread inside the Roti Babi. Leave some space at the opening so that it can be easily closed and sealed later.

Egg Coating

Beat the eggs and milk until frothy in a soup plate big enough to contain the Roti Babi.

Press the opening of each slice of stuffed bread together to prevent the filling from falling out. Dip the cut edge of the bread into the egg mixture first and press together to seal the slit. Now dip the three other edges and the two sides of the bread into the mixture, making sure that every part of the bread is covered.

Deep Frying

Heat up the oil. To test whether the oil is hot enough, drop in a small crust of bread into the oil. If it sizzles, the oil is ready for frying. The oil must be very hot, otherwise the Roti Babi will absorb too much oil.

First, immerse the slit edge of the Roti Babi into the hot oil to seal it. This is to ensure that the filling does not come out and also to prevent oil from entering the Roti Babi. Now put the Roti babi into the oil.

Remove from the oil when light brown. Remember that the bread will continue cooking after it has been taken out from the oil, so do not overcook. Drain the oil with the slit edge facing down so that the oil does not flow into the Roti Babi. Use kitchen tissue to absorb the excess oil.

Serve with Worcester sauce and thinly sliced red chillies.

This is the Roti Babi served in our family. The pockets in thick slices of bread are stuffed with minced pork cooked with onions, mushrooms and yambean. The stuffed bread is then coated with beaten egg and deep-fried.

GULAI TUMIS
(Serves 10 with other dishes)

This is a Nonya fish curry of Malay origin. *Gulai* is 'curry' in Malay and *tumis* is the Malay word used to describe the process of frying ground spices (*rempah*) in oil. This is, by tradition, done in an earthen pot (*belangah* in Malay or *chatty* in Tamil) until the oil separates from the *rempah* and is fragrant. Traditionally, homemade coconut oil is used.

Only the best fish – Tow Theh – is used. White Pomfret, its smaller relative, could also be used. Ikan Pari is a cheaper alternative. The ingredient that distinguishes this curry is bunga kantan, the bud of the torch ginger.

Gulai Tumis was served in various Hainanese establishments in Penang, including Loke Thye Kee at the corner of Burmah Road and Penang Road. Served with rice, it is accompanied by thinly sliced fried tanau kiam hu as a garnish. No vegetables like ladies fingers or brinjals are added, unlike some modern versions.

1 Tow Theh (large White Pomfret)
2 bunga kantan (torch ginger buds)

Rempah
3 stalks *serai* (lemongrass)
35 g dried chillies
60 g fresh red chillies
3 cloves garlic
120 g shallots
3 cm (30 g) kunyit (turmeric)
½ tbsp belacan, toasted

1½ tbsp (30 g) assam (tamarind), seeds removed
5 tbsp oil
4 tsp sugar
1 tsp salt, or to taste
1 litre water

Soak the tamarind in about 100 ml of water. Remove stray seeds if any. Squeeze the tamarind to separate the pulp from the fibres. Sieve to remove the fibres. Reserve the tamarind juice.

Cut the pomfret into about five pieces.

Cut off and discard the stem of the bunga kantan. Slice the pink bud into two, lengthwise, and then slice the bud finely (about 1.5 mm). Pound or grind all the *rempah* ingredients in a food processor.

Heat up the oil in *belangah*, a wok or a stainless steel pan. An aluminum pot may not be suitable because of the acidic tamarind. Fry the *rempah*, constantly stirring to ensure that it does not stick to the pot. Fry for about 15 minutes until the *rempah* is fragrant, the oil separates and the onions are transparent.

Add the assam juice, salt and remaining 900 ml of water. Stir and bring to the boil, then lower the heat and simmer for about 15 minutes.

Add the fish to the *gulai* and bring to a boil. Include the sliced bunga kantan and simmer for a few minutes until the fish is cooked. Remove some of the oil before serving. Most *gulai* taste better if eaten later in the day after they are cooked or the next day.

I am standing second from left with members of my family at a picnic at Telok Bahang.

HAINANESE SATAY BABI

Hainanese Satay is quite different from the Malay version. It is very distinct – the meat is more uniformly cut and the sauce is based on sweet potatoes instead of peanut and coconut milk. It is served with toasted bread and not with cucumber and onion as in the Malay style.

Traditionally, each stick of Hainanese Satay consists of two larger pieces of sliced lean pork with a thin strip of fat sandwiched in between – altogether three pieces – literally translated as *sa te* in Hokkien. This is as good an explanation as any for the generic name for this traditional Southeast Asian dish. There is another possible explanation. *Sathai* is a Tamil word meaning 'flesh'.

Satay is grilled over a charcoal fire. In my younger days, the skewers, or the satay sticks, were from the midribs of the coconut leaflets – called *lidi* in Malay or *lili* by the Penang Hokkiens. In more recent times the *lidi* has been replaced by imported bamboo skewers.

Hainanese Pork Satay is one of several types of Penang heritage food served at the then very popular Hainanese *kopi tiam* (coffee shop) 'next to Queens' in Penang Road. Queens was a theatre which was replaced by the Cathay cinema. It is now occupied by Mydin. Besides the pork satay or Satay Babi, you could also choose to have hoon cheang satay made from pig's small intestines. This is not so popular today.

Currently, there are not many places where you can get Hainanese satay with a good sweet potato sauce. When we were living in Irving Road, we had a Hainanese satay man who carried his wares on a *kandar* (pole). There was another satay man who went round the Pulau Tikus area on a tricycle. We used to wait eagerly for him – our own sliced bread at the ready – to come round every Thursday to Jones Road. He would brush the sliced bread with the oil, coconut milk and spice mixture and toast them after he had grilled the satay that we ordered. We could eat the hot sliced toast with just the satay sauce. Today, the same satay stall is parked at Bangkok Lane on Tuesday, Thursday and Saturday mornings. If he has any satay left in the afternoon, he goes back to the hawker area at *lau heok hnui* or sireh estate (Lengkok Burma), off Burnah Road next to the Shell Station. His is the best Hainanese Satay Babi that we can get in Penang.

There is another version of Satay Babi in other parts of Malaysia. It is served with a peanut sauce topped with a blob of grated pineapple.

For Satay Babi, it is best to use a lean cut like loin, otherwise more effort would be required in removing the sinews from the pork. An alternative is to use *twee bak* (thigh) which has some dense fat. In Malaysia and Singapore we can buy pork fat separately – for making lard and the crispy and tasty by-product, bak eu phok (fried lard cubes).

Satay Babi using traditional lidi *(mid-rib of coconut leaflet) instead of bamboo sticks.*

Hainanese Satay Babi
(Makes 50 sticks)

500 g lean pork
100 g pork fat
50 satay sticks (at least 15 cm long)
6 slices of bread

Marinade
1 clove garlic
2 stalks serai (lemongrass)
2.5 x 3 cm lengkuas (galangal)
3 tbsp thick coconut milk
3 tbsp coriander powder
2 tsp turmeric powder
2 tbsp light soya sauce
1 tbsp sugar
½ tsp salt

Sauce
150 g sweet potato
1 tbsp assam (tamarind) with seeds removed
5 dried chillies
1 small fresh chilli
500 ml water
2 x 3 cm lengkuas (galangal)
3 tbsp plum sauce
3 tbsp sugar, or to taste
½ tsp salt
1 tbsp light soya sauce

Basting Mix
1 tbsp oil
2 tbsp thick coconut milk
1 tbsp water
1 stalk lemongrass

Marinate
Peel, smash and chop up the garlic. Cut away and discard the leafy portion and roots of the lemongrass, leaving about 7 cm of the root ends. Peel away the fibrous sheath and slice finely. Skin the lengkuas and cut into smaller pieces.

Grind the garlic, lemongrass and lengkuas in a food processor or pound with a pestle and mortar (*lesong*) till very fine.

Thoroughly mix the coconut milk, coriander powder, turmeric powder, light soya sauce, sugar and salt together with the fresh ground spices.

Sauce
Clean the sweet potato, cut them into pieces and boil them in a pot of water till soft. Peel away the skin and mash the potato finely with a masher or food processor, adding water a little at a time if necessary.

Soak the assam in 50 ml of water for about 30 minutes. Squeeze the assam to separate the pulp from the fibre and seeds. Sieve to obtain assam juice. Soak the dried chillies without the stalks for at least 15 minutes and remove the seeds. Remove the stalks and seeds from the fresh chillies and slice. Grind the dried and fresh chillies in a food processor or pound till very fine.

Boil 500 ml of water and add the chilli paste. Simmer for about 10 minutes. Include the mashed potato and the rest of the sauce ingredients. Mix thoroughly and bring to the boil. Set aside.

Satay
Cut the lean pork into strips of about 3 x 2.5 cm, then cut across into slices about 3 or 4 mm thick.

Similarly, cut the pork fat into strips of about 3 x 2.5 cm, then into slices about 3 or 4 mm thick.

Marinate the lean pork and the fat for at least one hour or overnight in the refrigerator.

Soak the satay sticks in water for about half an hour to prevent the sticks from burning during the process of grilling. Skewer a piece of pork fat between pieces of lean pork on each satay stick. It is better to have five or seven alternating pieces of meat and fat instead of the traditional three if you are serving the satay as a main course rather than a starter.

Basting Mix
Add 2 tbsp thick coconut milk, 1 tbsp water and 1 tbsp oil to the left-over marinade to baste the satay during grilling.

Cut off the root of a stalk of lemongrass and crush the root end to use as brush for basting.

Grilling
Grill the satay over a charcoal fire or under a grill. If a grill is used, it must be turned on and be hot before the satay is put under it. Baste one side of the satay, and when it is cooked, turn over, baste, and grill.

Brush each side of the bread with the basting mix. It will colour the bread yellow. Toast both sides.

Serve the satay hot with the toasted bread and the satay sauce.

The Hainanese satay man outside our house in Irving Road in the early Fifties. The satay man in Bangkok Lane today has an uncanny resemblance to the old man. They even use the same fan!

Root end of a lemongrass stalk smashed and used as a basting brush for Satay Babi.

INDIAN INFLUENCE

ONE OF THE MORE IMPORTANT Indian influences on Penang food came with the large-scale immigration of Tamils, both Hindus and Muslims, to Penang from Southern India and Sri Lanka. This occurred in the late 19th and early 20th centuries. A precursor of this wave were Indian convict labourers sent to the penal colony of Penang from 1795 to 1806. Centuries earlier, Indian influence had already asserted itself on Malay cooking with the introduction of seed spices like cumin, fennel and coriander through Tamils trading in Southeast Asia.

Many of the Tamil Muslim immigrants were Malayalees from the Malabar coast in Southwest India. In Penang, they lived in Kampong Malabar and the nearby Malabar Street which were named after them. Malabar Street was later extended from the Penang Road end all the way to Beach Street and renamed Chulia Street as the Tamil Muslims were also referred to as Chulia Indians. There is still a sizable Indian community around the Beach Street end of Chulia Street. Interestingly, there is also a Chulia Street in Singapore. The Malayalees were well integrated into Malay culture and became known as Jawi Peranakan or Jawi Pekan. Indian Muslims are locally referred to as *mamak*, Tamil for 'uncle'.

The Tamil Muslims use more meat like mutton, chicken, fish and other seafood in their cooking compared to the Hindu Tamils. Vegetarian food predominates among the latter group who commonly use vegetables like peas, potatoes, carrots, eggplant (brinjal), okra, drumstick (buah kelor)*, cabbage and pulses like dhal and lentils in their cooking. My mother cooked a curry with drumstick, flower crab and taupok.

Coconut and coconut products like Gula Melaka (jaggery in Tamil), tamarind and curry leaves feature prominently in Tamil cooking. One basic Indian curry mix is garam masala which has as many variations as there are regions in the subcontinent. For South Indian food, turmeric and chillies are used, but for North Indian food, dry spices like black

* Buah kelor or drumstick is the fruit of a tree which is common in Southern India and Sri Lanka. As its name suggests, the fruit is long and slender like a drumstick. The tree is also called horse radish tree because the root was used by Europeans in the tropics in colonial times as a poor substitute for horse radish. The young leaves from this tree can also be eaten.

pepper, cinnamon, clove and cardamom are used instead.

South Indian food is served in restaurants like Meerah and Hameediya in Campbell Street, Dawood in Queen Street and small stalls at the Chulia Street end of Penang Road. There is an old stall at the Kapitan Kling mosque at Jalan Kapitan Keling (formerly Pitt Street). Interestingly, the taste of South Indian food has not changed significantly over the years unlike other Penang Heritage food like Hainanese fare.

Roti Canai is a common food found all over Malaysia. It probably got its name from Chennai, formerly Madras, the capital of what is now Tamil Nadu state in India. In Singapore and many other places it is called Roti Prata. This is a South Indian bread as distinct from North Indian bread like Naan and Chapati. The Penangites' favourite cuisine of Roti Canai and Teh Tarik were Malabari food popularised by the petty traders in the Kampong Malabar area. There were many *mamak* stalls selling Roti Canai, curries, rice and Teh Tarek in a cul-de-sac off Penang Road, next to and parallel to Chulia Steet. There are still a few stalls there by the side of Jalan Dato Koyah, opposite Kampong Malabar.

Although some of these foods are, to some extent, similar to those found in other parts of Malaysia and Singapore, the preparation is more elaborate in Penang. Murtabak is a good example. In the Penang version, still served today at Hameediyah in Campbell Street, the filling is specially prepared from fresh ingredients. However, in other parts of Malaysia and Singapore, meats from curries are chopped up with onions and used as filling. Furthermore, the Penang Murtabak is served with pickled onions and cut chillies.

Mee Goreng (fried noodles in Malay) and Mee Rebus (boiled noodles in Malay) used to be sold from mobile hawker carts equipped with two Chinese charcoal stoves – one for blanching the noodles and the beansprouts and the other for frying the Mee Goreng. Indian earthen pots were used in the early days, but were later replaced by aluminum ones with flared lips and bulbous bodies. The Chinese wok was used for frying. The stalls were pushed along the streets or parked on the side of the road. One of the most well-known stalls was the one stationed at Kelawei Road, close to the Paramount Hotel. Malaysia's Agong from Kedah used to patronize this stall. The stall is now at Nagore Court. There was another very popular stall outside our house in Jones Road; the stallholders used to live in our neighbour's back garden. This stall has since moved to a *kopi tiam* in Pulau Tikus.

Mee Rebus and Mee Goreng are both truly multiracial fusion foods. It is prepared by the *mamak* using largely Chinese ingredients like Hokkien mee (noodles), beansprouts, fried soya bean cake (tau kua) and a chilli-based gravy with reconstituted dry cuttlefish. The gravy used for the Mee Rebus is sweet potato based and pounded dried seafood is added to give it the distinctive flavour. Boiled potato coated with a *sambal* sauce is used as garnishing.

Most of these ingredients – tau kua, boiled potato and cuttlefish – are used in Pasembor, another dish sold by the *mamak*. Pasembor is similar to the Chinese Chneh Hu (literally translated as 'green fish' in Penang Hokkien). In other parts of Malaysia, Pasembor is called Rojak which is quite different from the Penang Rojak. Penang Rojak is a fruit salad. My cousin has a theory that Mee Goreng and Mee Rebus evolved from Pasembor. Mee, the Chinese noodles, were added to provide more carbohydrate for the labourers who frequented the stalls. Later, other Chinese ingredients like soya bean cake and beansprouts were also included. The fresh mee, soya bean products and beansprouts are sold in the same stall in wet markets then and now.

Masala Vadai and Samosa are two popular snacks. Masala Vadai is a deep-fried dhal patty with sliced onions and chillies. It used to be sold by Indians with Pisang Goreng and Ubi Goreng. There were two stalls on Dato Kramat Road, one close to the Kuantan Road junction and the other on Market Cross junction that offered Masala Vadai.

When we were young, we used to buy a choice assortment of nuts, pulses and Muruku from the *kacang puteh* stalls operated by Tamils who plied the streets. The nuts were packed in cones made out of recycled pages of used exercise books. At that time each cone of *kacang puteh* costs 10 cents!

CLAY POT · BELANGA · CHATTY · BOK KENG

Indians, Malays and the Nonyas traditionally use clay pots for cooking curries, particularly those which have tamarind as an ingredient. This is because the acidic tamarind is believed to corrode metal pots and taint the food. Clay pots are called *chatty* in Tamil, *belanga* in Malay and *bok keng* in Penang Hokkien. These are made locally and are available in Little India in Queen Street in Penang and Serangoon Road in Singapore. As the quality control for these pots is not good, it is best to check that there is no leak before you pay for your pot. Bring a bottle of water for the test!

You need to run in your clay pot before you start cooking with it. My cousin, Sandy, gave me the following advice on running-in a clay pot:

Cook grated coconut over a slow fire in the pot stirring continuously with a *senduk* (ladle made from coconut shell) or a wooden spoon till the coconut is dark brown. Spread the coconut over the inner surface of the pot that is exposed to the heat from the stove. Ensure that the coconut is not unduly burnt. Add water to cover the cooking area and a small handful of raw rice, and bring to a boil. Cover and simmer for about half an hour and turn off the heat. Leave the pot over night before cleaning it. Your *belanga* is now ready for use.

NASI KANDAR

The name Nasi Kandar comes from *kandar*, the wooden pole used by *mamak* hawkers to balance two containers or baskets containing rice and curries. As everything had to be carried around, the selection of curries they served was limited. Some of these hawkers settled in a fixed location. One of the better-known stalls is the one just outside Kapitan Kling Mosque in Pitts Street. Whenever my uncles return to Penang, they would go to this Nasi Kandar stall which offers a wide choice of *mamak* curries with vegetables like okra, brinjals, and dhals. Nasi Kandar dishes are also served at Merah, Hameediyah and Dawood.

Nasi Kandar is similar to what is known as Nasi Padang from Padang, Sumatra, where South Indian influence had prevailed for many centuries. The east coast of peninsula Malaysia have something similar in Nasi Dagang.

The fish curry my mother cooked must have been strongly influenced by the fish curry from the Nasi Kandar stall.

An hawker with baskets on a kandar (pole).

FISH CURRY

This is the fish curry cooked by my mother that we call Kelinga Gulai, a combination of words from different local languages that is typical of the Penang Hokkien dialect. *Kelinga* means 'Indian' in Penang Hokkien, and refers to Kalinga, a republic that was in central-eastern India. *Gulai* is Malay for 'curry'.

This fish curry is one of the limited varieties of dishes served by the old-time Nasi Kandar hawkers. The South Indian influence in this dish is characterized by the use of the Indian curry leaves and seed spices like coriander, cumin and fennel which are finely ground after roasting to bring out the flavours. Unlike Malay *gulai* which uses fresh red chillies in the *rempah*, Kelinga Gulai uses dried chillies which are first fried and then ground. Another South Indian influence is the use of tamarind pulp and coconut milk to produce a both a sour and a *lemak* (creamy) taste.

My mother used to take her fresh ingredients across the road from our house to an Indian lady who ground them for her using the *batu giling*. For those living in Malaysia and Singapore, there are wet markets where we can still buy wet ground spices from the Indian *rempah* lady. You tell her what curry you are cooking and she will give you the right curry mix. In the Pualu Tikus market in Penang, the *rempah* lady is Chinese – a clear illustration of the integration of the different races in Malaysia where food is concerned.

In the old days, *rempah* costs tens of cents but these days it can set you back by a few dollars – how things have changed!

Today, we can grind our own spices using an electric grinder or even a coffee grinder. It is more convenient to grind a larger quantity of spices and freeze the *rempah* for future use. Stored in the freezer, *rempah* can keep for up to three months. Just make sure that the spice paste is at room temperature before cooking.

Black Pomfret or Bawal Hitam is traditionally used for this curry. Mackerel (Tenggiri) can also be used.

Ladies finger, sliced onions and curry leaves are integral parts of this fish curry. Although brinjals are often added, our home-cooked version omits it.

You can prepare this curry from scratch or go for convenience and use packaged coconut milk and commercial spice powders.

This old paper bag from Hameediyah Indian restaurant lists its menu which includes Fish Curry.

The old slateboard used in Hameediyah Restaurant to add up the cost of the meal.

Fish Curry
(Serves 10 with other dishes)

500 g Bawal Hitam (Black Pomfret)
1 tbsp (about 20 g) assam (tamarind) pulp, deseeded
½ coconut to give 200 g grated coconut or
    110 ml concentrated coconut milk
750 ml water
3 cloves garlic, skinned and sliced thinly
1 tsp mustard seeds
1 tsp fenugreek

3 Bombay onions (about 150 g),
    peeled and sliced thinly
5 cardamoms, smashed
2 sprigs curry leaves
1 stick cinnamon (about 3 cm)
200 g ladies finger, stalk and tip sliced off
4 green chillies, partially slit
3 tomatoes, quartered
5 stalks spring onions, cut into 3 cm lengths
3 eggs, hard-boiled
3 tbsp oil
2 tsp salt

Ground Spices
15 dried chillies (approx. 15 gm) or 3 tbsp chilli powder
5 tbsp coriander seeds
1 tsp jintan puteh (cumin)
1 tsp jintan manis (fennel)
½ tsp black peppercorns
1 tsp kunyit (tumeric) powder

Wrap the grated coconut in a muslin cloth and squeeze out about half a bowl (110 ml) of thick coconut milk. Set aside. Now mix the grated coconut with 250 ml of warm water and squeeze out the thin coconut milk. Repeat with a third and fourth squeeze after mixing with 250 ml of warm water for each squeeze. Alternatively, use 110 ml of concentrated pasteurised or UHT coconut milk that is now more readily available in the shops in Malaysia, Singapore and overseas. Mix 10 ml of the concentrated coconut milk with 750 ml of water to make up the thin coconut milk.

Soak the tamarind pulp in 50 ml of warm water for about 30 minutes. Squeeze the tamarind between fingers and sieve to separate the fibre which is to be discarded. Reserve the tamarind liquid.

Remove the stalks of the dried chillies and fry the chillies without oil for about 3 to 4 minutes. Watch that they do not turn brown. Soak in warm water.

Fry the coriander in a pot for about 4 minutes and use a food processor to grind it till fine. Fry the cumin and fennel for 3 to 4 minutes and grind finely. Grind the black pepper. I find that the seed spices can be made finer by pounding in a mortar and pestle. Alternatively use the same measure of ready ground chillies, coriander, fennel, cumin, turmeric and pepper. Blend the ground spices in a food processor with the soaked chillies and about 150 ml of water. Set aside the *rempah*.

If these separate spice powders are not available, you could use 50 gm of commercial fish curry powder with ½ tsp of ground pepper added. Mix the ground spices with about 150 ml of water. Render into a smooth *rempah* paste and set aside.

Slice the fish into pieces of about 1.5 cm thickness. Rub some 2 tsp of salt all over the slices of fish.

Fry the garlic with the oil till slightly brown and remove from pot. Then, using the same oil, fry the fenugreek till fragrant. Add the mustard seeds and fry for about half a minute. Now add the *rempah* and *tumis* or stir

till fragrant. This will take at least 5 minutes. It is important to stir the *rempah* otherwise it will stick to the pot and be burnt. Add 1 to 2 tbsp of water if the *rempah* is too dry.

Add sliced onions, the cardamom, curry leaves and cinnamon. Stir for about a minute. Include the tamarind liquid and the thin coconut milk and bring to the boil. Lower the flame and simmer for about 15 minutes, after which put in the ladies fingers, green chillies, spring onions, tomatoes, and the fish.

When the fish is cooked, add the thick coconut milk and the boiled egg. Turn off the heat when the curry boils.

Bawal Hitam or Black Pomfret is the species commonly used for fish curry.

BUAH KELOR
DRUMSTICK CURRY

Kelor is the Malay name for drumstick, the fruit of the legume tree *Moringa oleifera* that originated from India. Its name in Tamil is *muruggal*. The fruit, which has a roughly triangular cross-section, is green and about 40 to 50 cm long and about 2 cm in diameter. The outer part of the fruit is very fibrous and cannot be eaten. The edible parts are the seeds and the surrounding flesh. Therefore, if the fruit is too young or too old there won't be much to eat.

The way to eat drumstick is to chew it and discard the fibrous part. The drumstick should be peeled to remove the thin outer green layer to make it easier to chew! A more genteel way to eat the drumstick is to cut the drumstick along its length to open it up and to scrape off the fleshy part to eat. Then there is no need to peel off the outer layer.

A by-product of the seed is ben oil which is used in salads, for cooking and as a lubricant for fine machinery such as watches. The young leaves of the tree are eaten by the Malays, the Indians and the Indonesians. Research has shown that the leaves have a very high protein and calcium content, and are therefore especially useful to vegetarians. The tree has tuberous roots which were used by colonial Europeans as a replacement for horse radish. Hence, it is also sometimes known as the horse radish tree.

This Buah Kelor Curry is a coconut-milk based curry or *gulai lemak* in Malay. It is one of the early Nonya fusion dishes which borrowed elements from the Malays and the Indians – the *buah kelor* having Indian origins while the curry is Malay.

Traditional Malay curries use fresh ingredients like turmeric, lemongrass and belacan but the *rempah* for this dish also includes dried chillies and coriander, which makes it more South Indian. My cousin, Sandy, tells me that if you grind your own coriander for this dish, you should not toast the coriander seeds before grinding them. Other ingredients of this dish are pineapple and tau pok (bean curd puff).

I talked to many relatives to find out more about drumstick curries and I got a wide variety of answers. There are apparently many drumstick dishes besides the one that my mother used to cook. My cousins recalled a similar *lemak gulai* with drumstick, long beans, prawns and bittergourd stuffed with minced pork. There is also a Southern Nonya Masak Lemak Kelor from Singapore and Malacca which has drumstick, pork ribs and prawns. My uncle, Runny, described an interesting dry masala curry of flower crabs and drumstick which was cooked by my grandmother.

Flower crabs or cheek in Penang Hokkien live in intertidal estuaries, hiding under the sand during the day and coming out to feed at dusk. The male flower crabs have blue markings on their soft shells while the female are dull green. The male flower crabs have longer pincers.

Fishermen used to land their sampans in the morning with their catch of flower crabs at the beaches along Gurney Drive and Tanjong Bungah. We bought the crabs directly from them.

This curry can be cooked in a traditional Indian clay pot or in a wok. Prawns can be used instead of crabs or in addition to them.

A single buah kelor is unusual as the pods normally grow in bunches. The young leaves of the tree can also be eaten.

Buah Kelor
(Serves 10 with other dishes)

Rempah
2 stalks lemongrass
10 dried chillies
10 shallots (about 100 g)
1 tbsp ground tumeric
3 tbsp ground coriander
1 tsp belacan

4 flower crabs
3 buah kelor (drumstick)
200 g long beans
100 g tau pok (bean curd puffs)
¼ small pineapple
4 tbsp oil
1 coconut to give 400 g grated coconut
    or 220 ml thick coconut milk
750 ml water
2 tsp salt

Rempah
Trim off and discard the leafy part of the lemongrass. Peel off the tough bits of the root end and slice the core thinly, stopping when the stalk becomes woody.

Break up the chillies and remove the seeds if you don't like your curry too spicy. Soak the dried chillies in water for about 10 minutes. Peel the shallots and cut them into wedges. Toast the belacan, breaking it up if necessary.

Pound these ingredients, starting with the lemongrass, the soaked dried chillies, shallots, ground turmeric, ground coriander and toasted belacan. Alternatively, use a food processor to liquidize, adding about 100 ml of water for the liquidizer to grind effectively. Reserve the *rempah*.

Wash the crabs and remove the bottom plates. Clean out the spongy tissues and chop each crab into two.

Wash the drumsticks and cut into lengths of about 3 cm. You can peel off the dark outer layer of the skin.

Wash the long beans. Discard the tips of each bean and break the beans into lengths of about 3 cm.

Cut the tau pok into two or four depending on their size.

Skin and remove the 'eyes' of the pineapple. Remove the core of the pineapple and cut the pineapple into two, lengthwise. Slice into pieces of about 1 cm thickness.

Wrap the grated coconut in a muslin cloth and squeeze out about a bowl (about 220 ml) of thick coconut milk. Set aside. Now mix the grated coconut with 250 ml of warm water and squeeze out the thin coconut milk. Repeat with a third and fourth squeeze after mixing with 250 ml of warm water for each squeeze.

Alternatively, use 220 g of concentrated pasteurised or UHT coconut milk that are now more readily available in the shops in Malaysia, Singapore and overseas. Mix 20 g of the concentrated coconut milk with 750 ml of water to make up the thin coconut milk.

Heat up a pot or wok and, when sufficiently hot, put in the 4 tbsp of oil. *Tumis* or fry the *rempah* till it is fragrant and the oil separates. Add 1 - 2 tbsp of water gradually if it is too dry.

Add the drumsticks and mix with the *rempah*. Now pour in the thin coconut milk and bring to a boil. Include the crabs and bring to a boil again before adding the pineapple, the tau pok and the long beans.

Bring to a boil once again, then lower the heat to simmer for about 15 minutes. Finally, pour in the thick coconut milk. Stir to mix well and turn off the heat before it boils. Serve with rice.

Pineapple, long beans, shallots and, of course, buah kelor or drumstick are some of the ingredients of this tasty curry with different flavours and textures.

Mee Goreng is a fried noodle dish prepared by South Indians using predominantly Chinese ingredients.

MEE GORENG & MEE REBUS
INDIAN NOODLES
KELINGA MEE

Kelinga Mee in Penang Hokkien dialect means Indian noodles, referring to two popular Penang hawker dishes – Mee Rebus and Mee Goreng. Although referred to as Indian, you wouldn't find these dishes in India because these are two early truly Penang fusion foods. Mee Rebus means 'boiled noodles' while Mee Goreng is 'fried noodles' in Malay. These are two dishes traditionally prepared by South Indian Muslims (or *mamak*) in their mobile push-carts, using predominantly Chinese ingredients such as noodles, beansprouts and tau kwa (soyabean cake). The yellow noodles used is a variety referred to as Hokkien mee or sek mee. *Sek* means 'cooked' in Hokkien and refers to this noodle being sold pre-cooked. Garnishes of boiled curried potatoes, fried tau kwa, curried cuttlefish and Gneow Chu Chnee are added. Gneow Chu Chnee is so called because it resembles a small mouse or *gneow chu* in Penang Hokkien. It is made of a dough of self-raising flour, minced dried prawns or anchovies and deep fried in oil. These garnishes are also used in another *mamak* dish called Pasembor.

The most well-known Mee Rebus and Mee Goreng push-cart stall in Penang used to be stationed outside the Paramount Hotel at Northam Road (Jalan Sultan Ahmad Shah). It boasts the patronage of the Sultan of Kedah who was then Malaysia's Agong. The stall moved to the Chinese Recreation Club in Victoria Green and more recently to Nagore Court.

For many years, we had a Kelinga Mee push-cart stationed outside our house in Jones Road. We used to bring our own plates and eggs for the hawkers to boil and add to the Mee Rebus. In those days, Mee Rebus and Mee Goreng cost 30 cents a plate. The hawkers lived at the back of our neighbour's house. My mother used to pass dead branches that had been pruned from our trees to the hawkers for them to use as firewood. When our neighbour moved away, the stall moved to Tip Top Café at Pulau Tikus. It later moved to the coffee shop at the junction of Jalan Pasar and Moulmeim Road.

Before they were based outside our house, the Indian noodle push-cart hawkers used to ply a route around the Pulau Tikus area, ending at Gurney Drive in the evening. They would stop at any point to take orders and prepare the dishes. The push-cart was self-sufficient, carrying everything from the ingredients to water to wash the dishes. There were two charcoal stoves at one end of the push-cart, one for the pot of boiling water to blanch the noodles and the beansprouts and another for the *kuali* or the wok for frying the Mee Goreng. The work area where the garnishes were sliced and the dishes were prepared was simply the pavement. Interestingly, the present stall in the coffee shop is not very different from the original push-cart.

Mee Rebus is basically Hokkien mee and beansprouts blanched in boiling water and served with garnishes. It is topped with a potato-based gravy, cuttlefish gravy, and chilli paste if you like your Mee Rebus spicy hot. A boiled egg is optional. There are other types of Mee Rebus gravies, one of which includes pounded groundnuts. These versions are normally sold by Malay hawkers.

Mee Goreng is the fried version of Kelinga Mee. The noodles, beansprouts and garnishes are fried with the gravy from the cuttlefish and chilli sauce if preferred. Egg is another optional ingredient. Unlike the Mee Goreng from some other parts of Malaysia and Singapore, tomato sauce is generally not used in Penang. The gravy from the cuttlefish is what gives the Mee Goreng its special taste. I like my Mee Goreng with some Mee Rebus gravy. Don't hesitate to ask as it is a common practice in Penang.

Both Mee Rebus and Mee Goreng are topped with sliced lettuce, fried sliced shallot, sliced green chllies and a wedge of lime. Those prepared by hawkers tends to have little or no meat. If you like meat in Mee Rebus and Mee Goreng, you could add beef. This would provide more flavour to the chilli sauce as, in this recipe, the beef is simmered in the sauce.

This recipe is based on the Mee Rebus and Mee Goreng served from the push-cart outside our house. The gravy and the garnishes are prepared first, starting with the chilli paste. The chilli paste is divided into five portions – two portions are used for the cuttlefish, one portion for the boiled potatoes/chilli sauce and two portions for the Mee Rebus gravy. The excess chilli sauce for the boiled potatoes is used to spice up the Mee Rebus and Mee Goreng if you like your dish spicy hot.

As the cuttlefish has to be soaked overnight in water, and after that in the lye solution for eight hours, it has to be prepared at least one day before it is required.

In the *mamak* stall you could choose to have Mee Rebus, Mee Goreng or both. Mee Rebus gravy could be added to Mee Goreng, if preferred. Mee Goreng is best eaten hot, fresh from the frying pan.

Rebus means 'boiled', so Mee Rebus is a boiled noodle dish.

Mee Goreng Rempah, Gravy & Garnishes
(Serves 10)

Rempah
3 tbsp chilli powder
5 fresh red chillies
2 tsp ground turmeric
250 g Bombay onions or shallots
3 tbsp oil
250 ml water

5 tbsp chilli powder
8 fresh red chillies
3½ tsp ground turmeric
400 g Bombay onions or shallots
5 tbsp oil
400 ml water

Cuttlefish and Gravy
100 gm dried cuttlefish
1 tsp kan sui (lye crystals) or sodium bicarbonate
1 tbsp assam (tamarind) with 50 ml water
2 portions of the chilli paste prepared earlier
1 tbsp salt
2 tbsp sugar
600 ml water

Remove the stalks of the fresh chillies, slit the chillies open and discard the seeds if you don't want your chilli paste to be too hot. Cut the chillies into pieces. Peel the onions and chop each into eighths.

Grind the onions, the chopped chillies, the chillie powder and ground turmeric in a food processor till fine. Add about 50 ml of water to ensure that the *rempah* circulates so that the ingredients are ground effectively. Set the *rempah* aside.

Heat up a wok. When it is hot, add the oil and fry the *rempah* for about 10 - 15 minutes till fragrant. Add 1 - 2 tbsp of water gradually when the *rempah* becomes dry. When fragrant, add the rest of the water. Bring to a boil, lower the flame and simmer for about 5 minutes.

Divide the chilli paste into three portions – two portions for the cuttlefish and one portion for the potatoes. Keep aside.

Variation: If you, like me, prefer Mee Goreng with Mee Rebus gravy, increase the quantity of chilli paste ingredients to the following to make the gravy. Divide the chilli paste into five portions – two for Mee Rebus gravy, two for the cuttlefish and one for the potatoes.

Wash the cuttlefish and soak in 600 ml water overnight. Keep the water as stock for later use.

Dissolve the lye crystals or bicarbonate of soda in sufficient water to cover the cuttlefish. Soak the cuttlefish in the lye solution for about eight hours to soften them. Discard the water, rinse the cuttlefish and soak in water for another hour and then rinse again.

Soak the tamarind in the 50 ml of water. Squeeze the tamarind between the fingers and sieve to separate the pulp from the fibre which is to be discarded. Reserve the tamarind liquid. If you are making Mee Rebus Gravy to have with your Mee Goreng, prepare double the portion of tamarind liquid and save half for the Mee Rebus gravy.

Boil two portions of the chilli paste prepared earlier with the cuttlefish, the tamarind water, the water used to soak the cuttlefish, the salt and the sugar. Simmer for about half an hour.

Cut the cooked cuttlefish into ½ cm slices to use as a garnish. Reserve the cuttlefish gravy for later use.

Curried Potatoes and Beef

500 gm potatoes
One portion of chilli paste prepared earlier
2 tsp salt
300 gm stewing beef, optional
500 ml water

Boil the potatoes with skin on for 15 to 20 minutes till nearly cooked. Drain the water and peel the potatoes.

Boil the chilli paste with the 500 ml water, salt and sugar to make the hot chilli sauce.

Cut the beef into slices of about 1.5 cm thickness. Add the beef to the chilli sauce prepared earlier. Simmer for about 45 minutes (or less if a good cut of beef is used). Remove the beef slices. Slice thinly.

Add the boiled potatoes to the remaining chilli sauce and bring to the boil. Turn off the heat and leave aside for at least half an hour for the potatoes to absorb the sauce. Remove the potatoes, leaving behind the sauce, and cut them into slices for garnishing. Set aside the chilli sauce to spice up the Mee Rebus and the Mee Goreng if preferred.

If Beef is Not Used

Reduce the volume of water to 250 ml make the chilli sauce if beef is not used.

Gneow Chu Chnee

10 g dried prawns
15 g shallots
100 g self-raising flour
    or 100 g flour with ½ tsp baking powder
2 tbsp ground rice
1 egg, beaten
¼ tsp salt
100 ml water
Oil for deep frying

Pound or grind the dried prawns in a food processor. Peel the shallots and chop them up finely.

Mix the flour, ground rice and baking powder and sieve into a mixing bowl. Add the beaten egg, salt and the ground prawns and gradually add the water, stirring continuously with a wooden spoon till a consistent mixture is obtained. Add the chopped shallots, and knead into a soft dough.

Divide the dough mixture into 10 portions and fashion each portion into an ovoid. Sieve some flour over the Gneow Chu Chnee to make it easier to handle. Deep fry in hot oil till brown. Drain.

Other Garnishes

Soya bean cake (tau kwa), shallow fry till brown on
    both sides. Sliced into 2 and cut across into slices
    about 3 mm thickness.
Fried sliced shallots
200 g lettuce, finely sliced (about ½ cm)
2 limes, cut into wedges
5 fresh green chillies, thinly sliced

Gneow chu chnee.

Mee Goreng
(Serves 10)

Like Penang Char Kway Teow, it's best to prepare Mee Goreng in individual portions. This is especially important at home where you can only turn the heat of the stove up to a certain point. This method is for frying one serving at a time. (See pages 154-155 for gravy, *rempah* and garnishes.)

1 kg Hokkien mee (fresh yellow noodles)
600 g beansprouts

For each portion of Mee Goreng
4 tbsp cuttlefish gravy
1 tsp light soya sauce
1 or 2 tbsp chilli gravy according to taste
½ tsp sugar
1 egg
2 tsp oil

Boil about 3 litres of water in a pot and add 500 g of the noodles. Stir, and, before the water boils again, pour the noodles into a colander placed over another pot. Pour the noodles back into the first pot and fill it with a generous amount of cold water. Rinse the noodles and pour back into colander. This will ensure that the blanched noodles do not stick together. Repeat to blanch the other 500 g of the noodles.

Heat up a wok and then add 1 tsp of the oil. When the oil is hot, add one portion each of the bean sprouts and the noodles. Include the cuttlefish gravy, light soya sauce and the chilli gravy according to taste. Fry to mix the ingredients well.

Add the garnishes of sliced fried soyabean cake, cuttlefish, boiled potatoes, beef (if using), and Gneow Chu Chnee. Stir fry for about two minutes.

Move the noodles to the side of the wok to make a well in the centre. Add one teaspoon of oil, crack in the egg and stir. When the egg is partially scrambled, combine it with the noodles.

Dish out and serve with sliced lettuce, fried sliced shallots and a wedge of lime.

Mee Goreng is best eaten hot, fresh from the frying pan. Mee Rebus gravy can be added, if preferred.

Mee Goreng stall, circa 1950 (Penang Museum Collection)

Jones Road Mee Goreng at the stall at Moulmein Road.

Mee Rebus

(Serves 10)

Traditionally, Mee Rebus is prepared individually, plate by plate. Portions of the noodles and beansprouts are placed in a woven bamboo colander ladle and blanched in a pot of boiling water.

The beansprouts for the Mee Goreng are fried with the noodles but for Mee Rebus, the beansprouts should be blanched in a generous volume of boiling water.

Prepare chilli paste, cuttlefish and gravy, curried potatos, Gneow Chu Chnee and other garnishes as for Mee Goreng (see pages 155 and 156).

1 kg Hokkien mee (fresh yellow noodles)
600 g beansprouts, blanched
5 boiled eggs, each cut into 8

Mee Rebus Gravy
500 g sweet potatoes
1 tbsp assam (tamarind) with 100 ml water
300 g tomatoes
50 g dhal, soaked in water for 3 hours
50 g dried prawns
50 g Ikan Bilis (Whitebait)
1 tsp ground turmeric
3 cm cinnamon stick
3 cardamoms
2 portions of chilli paste prepared earlier
1 tbsp sugar
1 tbsp salt
1.5 litres water

Clean and peel the sweet potatoes, cut them into chunks and boil till soft. (Insert a knife into each of them to test for softness.) Mash the sweet potatoes thoroughly with a masher.

Soak the tamarind in the 100 ml of water. Squeeze the tamarind between fingers and sieve to separate the pulp from the fibre which is to be discarded. Reserve the tamarind liquid.

Rinse and soak the dhal for about 3 hours. Wash and cut tomatoes into quarters.

Pound or grind the dried prawns and Ikan Bilis in a food processor. If a food processor is used, add about 50 ml water. Fry without oil in a wok till fragrant. Keep aside.

Pound finely or blend in a food processor the dhal that has been soaked in water. Add about 50 ml water if using a food processor to ensure that it is well blended.

Put the ground dried prawns, Ikan Bilis, the pounded dhal, the ground turmeric, tomatoes, cinnamon stick and cardamom pods in a pot. Add the water and bring to boil. Simmer for about 10 minutes. Add the two portions of the chilli paste prepared earlier.

Add the mashed sweet potatoes, sugar and salt. Mix thoroughly in a food processor. Bring to a boil and simmer for about 5 minutes. The Mee Rebus gravy is ready for serving. It does not have to be served hot.

Into individual dishes, place some beansprouts then noodles. Spread, on top, the garnishes of sliced fried tau kwa, cuttlefish, boiled potatoes, Gneow Chu Chnee and boiled egg. Slices of beef can also be added.

Pour a ladle of the Mee Rebus gravy and 1 tablespoon of the cuttlefish gravy over the ingredients. Add the remaining chilli sauce from preparing the potato if you like your Mee Rebus spicy hot.

Add the sliced lettuce and sprinkle on the fried sliced shallots and sliced green chillies. Serve with a wedge of lime. Mee Rebus can also be served buffet style.

Roti Canai is known as Roti Prata in Singapore. The secret to making good Roti Canai is to enclose as much air in the pastry as possible, which is the reason why the dough is stretched and twirled.

ROTI CANAI
(Makes 6)

Roti Canai is eaten for breakfast and lunch. It can simply be eaten with sugar or it can be served with Dalcha, a simple curry made of vegetables like onions, potatoes, carrot, eggplant, tomatoes and green chillies, cooked with dhal. Often, bones and fat from mutton or lamb are added to give it more taste. If you are lucky, you may find a few scraps of meat attached to the bones, or the fat. You could also have an egg fried with your Roti Canai, but this was not so common in my youth because eggs were relatively expensive then. Still, it was and remains an inexpensive meal which costs less than a bowl of noodles. However, in higher-end stalls it is served with various meat curries.

The key component of Roti Canai is the dough which is stretched by swinging or flipping into a thin filo pastry.

My best early recollection of Roti Canai was the square one, made by folding four sides of the stretched dough to form an envelope. A more complicated technique is to loosely roll the stretched dough into a long thin cylinder, and to twist it into a 'rope' which is then fashioned into a circle by making a spiral. Whatever method is employed, the secret for making good Roti Canai, like other puff pastries, is to enclose as much air in the pastry as possible.

After frying in oil or ghee, the Roti Canai is taken back to the work surface and compacted by hand several times in a clapping action. This is to fluff up the pastry.

400 g flour
1 egg
1 tsp salt
1 tbsp sugar
1 tbsp condensed milk
1 tsp ghee
130 ml hot water
Oil for coating dough and frying pastry

Beat the eggs and add the salt, sugar, the condensed milk and the ghee. You may replace ghee with oil. Mix well.

Sieve the flour on a smooth surface or worktop. Make a well in the middle and add the egg mixture. Work the egg mixture with the surrounding flour using your fingers. Add the water and gradually draw in the flour to form the dough. Use the palm of one hand to push the mixture and the fingers of the other to stretch it by pulling back. Knead the dough for about ten minutes or until the dough does not stick to the hand nor the work surface.

Some flours absorb more water than others, so add water a little at a time if the dough is too stiff. The dough should be soft so that it spreads out on the worktop when pressed. If the dough is too wet, drizzle some more flour and knead.

Alternatively, a food processor with a dough hook can be used. It is will save much time and effort. Mix half the sieved flour with the ingredients and the water. Replace the mixing blade of the food processor with a dough hook and add the flour a little at a time until the dough is formed. The dough is ready when the dough separates from the container. Remove the dough from the dough hook and knead on a worktop for about two minutes.

Divide the dough into six equal portions. Liberally coat the dough with about 1 tbsp oil and place it in a bowl. Cover the bowl and leave for at least eight hours or overnight in the fridge.

Spread about ½ tsp to 1 tsp of oil on a smooth work surface and flatten one of the small balls of dough with your hand to spread it out evenly into a circle. Then stretch it out to obtain a thinner pastry by holding the edge of the pastry and pulling it further outwards and pressing it down on the surface to prevent the edge of the pastry from shrinking back. Repeat all around the perimeter of the pastry. Stretch the pastry to about 14 cm in diameter. A hole may appear in the pastry if a particular area is over-stretched. Don't worry, for Roti Canai it doesn't matter.

To make a simple, square version of Roti Canai, fold four sides of the stretched pastry inward to form a square envelope. A more complex method is to spread oil over the stretched pastry, then pinch the edge of the pastry and, while pulling it up, twirl it to form a rope. Use this rope to form a small circular spiral of pastry and flatten into a larger circle. Leave aside for about 5 minutes

Repeat for the remaining portions of the dough.

Fry the Roti Canai in a hot pan or griddle with 1 tsp of oil or ghee till slightly brown and crispy. Flip over to fry the other side. Transfer the fried Roti Canai to the worktop and compact it a few times with a clapping motion. It is ready to be served!

MURTABAK

Murtabak is another early Malaysian fusion food based on the thin filo pastry used in Roti Canai. Some smart alec must have thought, why don't we add a sprinkle of onions and bits of meat? This is probably how the Murtabak evolved from the egg Roti Canai. Nowadays we get a variety of Murtabak fillings like cheese, sardines and bananas although the original filling is made of egg, spicy meat and onions.

Murtabak is prepared by Indian Muslims (*mamak*) who originated from South India. This dish is unique to Malaysia and Singapore and is not likely to be found in India. The Penang Murtabak, like so many Penang dishes, is more complex compared to the versions from Kuala Lumpur or Singapore.

The key component of Murtabak is the dough which is stretched by flipping it into a thin filo pastry. In the Penang version, the stretched pastry is folded into a square and fried on both sides on an oil-coated griddle. A mixture of beaten eggs and a pre-cooked filling of spices, minced meat and diced onions are then spread on the pastry.

Once this preparation is cooked, it is flipped over and the pastry is similarly covered with the filling on the other side. When both sides are cooked, it is removed from the griddle and placed in the middle of a large thinly stretched pastry. The filling is wrapped in the pastry like an envelope and returned to the griddle and fried till brown on both sides. When the finished Murtabak is cut we get a sandwich of a crispy, thin pastry, the filling, the thick pastry base and then the filling and thin pastry again. Murtabak is best eaten fresh from the griddle when it is still crispy.

In Penang, Murtabak is served with sliced pickled onions and various curry sauces. The recipe for the pickled onions is given here, and you might wish to prepare the fish curry on page 145 to go with Murtabak. Otherwise, open a can of curry from the supermarket!

There were once two stalls in Campbell Street which served excellent Murtabak – Meerah and Hameediyah. We always go to Hameediyah. Sadly, Meerah and another stall that serves Murtabak at Pulau Tikus in the morning have also closed.

The Murtabak from Kuala Lumpur and Singapore (e.g at Zam Zam in Arab street) does not have the filling-coated pastry in the centre. The process starts with the stretched pastry. Diced raw onions and cooked minced meat are sprinkled in the middle of the pastry and egg is added and spread over. The four sides of the pastry are folded over to cover the filling to form an envelope. The envelope is transferred to a hot griddle for shallow frying. In several stalls in Kuala Lumpur, instead of minced meat, they chop up rather coarsely whatever meat you request from one of their curries.

This Murtabak recipe is the one which I adapted from my second aunt's recipe when I lived in London in the Seventies.

The Murtabak we used to eat were bigger. As with many hawker food, the portions have become smaller with time due to inflation. However, I have made the individual size of the Murtabak smaller here so that it is easier to prepare.

Murtabak
(Makes 8)

Filling

450 g minced mutton
2 cm ginger
50 g shallots
5 onions (approx. 250 gm)
5 cloves garlic
1 tbsp chilli powder
1 tsp kunyit (turmeric) powder
2 tbsp curry powder
2 sprigs mint, finely chopped
2 sprigs coriander leaves, finely chopped
½ tsp salt
8 eggs
1 tbsp oil

Pickled Onions

200 g red onions
1 green chilli
4 tbsp vinegar
1 tbsp sugar
Pinch of salt

Pastry

450 g flour

1 egg
1 tsp salt
1 tbsp sugar
1 tbsp condensed milk
1 tsp ghee
Oil for coating dough and frying pastry,
    'omelette' and Murtabak
140 ml hot water

Filling

Chop up the ginger and squeeze out the juice. Set the ginger juice aside. Peel the shallots and chop finely. Peel and dice the onions. Set aside. Peel and chop up the garlic.

Mix the chilli, turmeric and curry powders with 4 tbsp of water into a smooth spice paste.

Fry the sliced shallots in 1 tbsp of oil till brown. Add the spice paste and stir for about a minute. Include the minced mutton and stir continuously until the mutton browns.

Finally, put in the onions and fry till they just become transparent. Add the mint, ginger juice and the coriander. Set the filling aside.

Divide the filling into eight portions.

Pickled Onion Garnish

Prepare this garnish ahead of time. Peel and slice the red onions thinly. Slice the chillies. Mix the vinegar with the sugar and salt, then add the sliced onions and chillies to the mixture.

Pastry

Beat the eggs and add the salt, sugar, the condensed milk and the ghee. Mix well.

Sieve the flour on a smooth surface or worktop. Make a well in the middle of the flour and add the egg mixture. Work the egg mixture with the surrounding flour using your fingers. Add the water and gradually draw in the flour to form the dough. Use the palm of one hand to push the mixture and the fingers of the other to stretch it by pulling back. Knead the dough for about ten minutes or until the dough does not stick to the hand or the work surface.

Some flours absorb more water than others, so you may have to add more water a little at a time if the dough is too stiff. The dough should be soft such that it spreads out on the worktop when pressed. If the dough is too wet, drizzle some more flour and knead.

Alternatively, a food processor with a dough hook can be used. It is will save much time and effort. Mix half the sieved flour with the ingredients and the water. Replace the mixing blade of the food processor with a dough hook and add the flour a little at a time until the dough is formed. The dough is ready when the dough separates from the container. Remove the dough from the dough hook and knead on a worktop for about 2 minutes

Divide the dough into eight equal portions. Divide each portion into two parts, one double the size of the other. You should therefore have eight large balls and eight small balls of dough. The smaller ones are for the square base for the filling and the larger ones are for wrapping the fillings in.

Liberally coat the balls of dough with about 1 table-spoon of oil and place the dough in a bowl. Cover and leave for at least eight hours or overnight in the fridge.

Murtabak Filling

Spread about ½ tsp to 1 tsp of oil on a smooth work surface and flatten one of the small balls of dough with your hand to spread it out evenly into a circle. Then stretch it out to obtain a thinner pastry by holding the edge of the pastry and pulling it further outwards and pressing it down on the surface to prevent the edge of the pastry from shrinking back. Repeat all around the parameter of the pastry. Stretch the pastry to about 14 cm in diameter. A hole may appear on the pastry if a particular area is over-stretched. If the hole is too big, gather the dough together, re-form into a ball, knead and start again.

Fold the four sides of the pastry to form a square of approximately 14 x 14 cm. Fry this in a pan with a about 1 tsp of oil. Flip over when it is brown to fry the other side. Prepare all the bases and stack them one on top of another. Set aside.

Inner Murtabak Filling

Beat one egg and mix in one portion of the spiced mutton mixture. Heat up a pan, add 1 tsp of oil and place a prepared pastry on the pan. Spread half the filling on the pan to make a square about the same size as the pastry. Place the square pastry over the filling and spread another half of the filling on top of the pastry. When the filling is brown, carefully turn over to cook the other side.

Oil your worktop with about 1 tsp of oil and flatten a big ball of dough which you have prepared earlier. Use the process as for the smaller dough ball to make a thin sheet of pastry. The diameter of this wrapping pastry should be about 20 cm.

Place a cooked filling-coated pastry in the centre of the wrapping pastry. Fold the four edges of the wrapping pastry over the filling and return the envelope to the hot griddle, with the side with the flaps downwards. Drizzle about 1 tsp oil around the Murtabak. When one side is browned, flip over to fry the other side. Remove from the griddle when the pastry is crispy and golden brown.

Repeat for the remaining ingredients.

Cut into strips about 2 cm wide and serve with the pickled onions and a curry sauce. Best eaten hot.

The cumin seeds in the pastry add flavour of my wife's Samosas. They are always popular when she serves them.

SAMOSA
(Makes 20)

The savourySamosa that we are familiar with in Penang and other parts of Malaysia and Singapore originated in India. However, its origins go back further in time to the 9th century and further away westwards to Central Asia. Sanbosag or Sanbusaj is the Persian name for Samosa. Similar pronunciations are still current in Egypt, Syria and Lebanon.

Ground meat, especially lamb, has been used for the filling. There are also savoury and sweet vegetarian versions. The Turkish equivalent is called Borek. Its filo-like pastry has savory fillings like cheese or potato. Samosas today have fillings of minced lamb as the main ingredient with potatoes, onions and spices. The vegetarian version is stuffed with potatoes, onions and other vegetables like carrots, peas and cauliflower, with spices and ginger. The filling used in the different types of curry puffs found in Malaysia and Singapore must relate to the Samosa.

Traditionally, Samosas are triangular or conical in shape. In Central Asia, they are also made in a half-moon shape similar to our Nonya curry puffs and the Malay Epok-Epok. The envelope to wrap up the Samosa filling is made up of a dough of flour, water and fat (ghee, butter, margarine, lard or vegetable oil). Whole cumin seeds are added as well so that when you chew into a seed you have a whiff of the cumin.

This is a vegetarian Samosa cooked by my wife. When she brings Samosas to any social function in London they disappear like magic. She used to make the pastry from this recipe. However, she has found it convenient to use frozen Poh Piah wrappers which are now readily available. It is surprisingly similar to filo-pastry used by the Turkish.

Pastry

125 g flour
50 g butter
¼ tsp salt
½ tsp cumin seeds
50 ml milk

Filling

120 g Bombay onion
140 g potatoes
120 g carrots
100 g peas
1 tbsp curry powder for vegetable or fish
2 tbsp milk
1 tsp salt
1 tsp oil
Oil for deep frying

Cut the onions into ½-cm cubes and break up into squares. Peel the potatoes and carrots and cut them into ½-cm cubes. Thaw the peas (if frozen) in water and drain. Mix the curry powder with 2 tbsp of water.

Sieve the flour and salt together. Rub the butter into the flour until it resembles fine breadcrumbs. Stir in the cumin seed, gradually add the milk and knead into a dough. It is ready when the dough separates from your hand. Cover with a damp cloth and leave to sit for 3 to 4 hours.

Knead the dough and divide into two or three portions and roll them out separately on a floured board until they are very thin. Cut out circles from the dough with the help of a saucer, bowl or tin with a diameter of approximately 12 cm. Gather the scraps of the dough and reform into a ball and roll out on the floured board until very thin. Cut out more circles. Cut each circle of dough into half and dust each with a bit of flour to prevent them from sticking together. Stack them up. Cover and leave the pastry aside.

Heat up a wok till hot. Spread 1 tsp of oil in the wok and add the curry paste. Stir in the onions and fry for about a minute. Add the carrots and potatoes and fry for

about 2 minutes or till the carrots are soft. Add about one or two tablespoons of water if too dry. Finally, add the peas, the milk, and stir for another 2 minutes. Add another one or two tablespoons water to the mixture if it becomes too dry or sticks to the wok. Turn off the heat and allow to cool.

Moisten the edge of a piece of pastry with water. Place the filling on one side of the pastry and fold over. Press the edges together to seal. There are many other ways of wrapping the filling to form a pyramid. The challenge is to put as much filling in the Samosa as possible so that there is no air pocket enclosed.

Repeat for the remaining ingredients and pastry.

Heat oil in a wok for deep frying. Fry the Samosas in batches for 2 to 3 minutes on both sides until they are golden brown. Drain on kitchen paper.

Two ways of wrapping Samosa.

MASALA VADAI
(Makes 20)

Masala Vadai is a deep-fried savoury snack that originated from South India. It is slightly spicy and made with dhal, sliced onions and chillies. We used to buy Masala Vadai from the Indian man who also sold Pisang Goreng (deep fried bananas), Ubi Goreng (deep fried sweet potato) and champedak (a variety of jackfruit), among other things. There used to be two stalls on Dato Kramat Road, one close to the Kuantan Road junction and the other on the opposite side of the road on Market Cross junction, near the General Hospital.

This is the vegetarian hawker version where the dhal is only partially ground, giving the vadai a bit of bite. There is another type of vadai which uses black gram or urad dhal. The *dhal* is more finely ground and prawns are added. Some of these are shaped like a doughnut. The Tamils eat their Masala Vadai with fresh green chillies; you take a bite of the vadai and then a bite of the chilli if you like it that way.

There are different types of dhals which can be used. It can be quite confusing because many dhals look the same. Dhals are pulses which are defined as annual leguminous plants that yield one to twelve seeds within a pod. The same pulse could have different names. For example kala chana is the smaller chickpea with the brown skin that is toasted and sold as Kacang Puteh in Malaysia and Singapore. However if the skin or hull of the pulse is removed and split into two it becomes a dhal. The same kala chana when split is called chana dhal.

Another confusion arises because of the different Indian regional names of dhals. *Chana* is a Hindi word for the pulse. As Masala Vadai is a South Indian snack and the majority of Indians in Malaysia and Singapore are Tamils, the dhals are locally known by their Tamil names. Chana dhal is called kadalai paruppu and kala chana is called kondai kadalai. Toor dhal or tuvaram paruppu (in Tamil) can also be used. Also known as yellow pigeon peas, it is smaller than chana dhal. Both these dhals are round while mung dhal is oval. The latter is the green bean used in Chinese cooking. Black gram or urad dhal is much like the green mung beans but it is black on the outside and white inside. Hence, husked urad dhal is called white lentils. The ground flour is used for Dosia and Idli commonly eaten by Tamils.

250 g chana dhal (gram dhal)
  or toor dhal (yellow pigeon peas)
3 medium-sized onions (about 125 g)
2 dried chillies or 1 tsp chilli powder
3 green chillies
3 sprigs curry leaves
1 tbsp ground rice or flour, optional
¼ tsp salt
1 tsp jintan manis (cumin)
Oil for frying

Wash and soak the dhal in a generous amount of water for about 4 hours. The dhal absorbs a fair amount of water. In hot weather it is better to keep it in the refrigerator especially if the dhal is soaked overnight.

Wash and soak the dried chillies for about 20 minutes. Remove the seeds from the dried chillies if you prefer your Masala Vadai to be less spicy. Pound in a mortar until you obtain a fine paste.

Rinse and drain the soaked dhal. Pound ¾ of the dhal to a fine paste. Mix the pounded dahl and chillies together. Alternatively use a electric blender to grind all the chillies and ¾ of the dhal together. Allow this batter to rest for about 20 minutes.

In the meantime, skin the onions and cut each one from stalk to root into two. Then cut each half into thirds and shred by cutting crosswise to a thickness of 2 to 3 mm.

Remove the stalks from the fresh green chillies and slice the chillies crosswise to a thickness of about 3 mm. Shake off and discard the seeds. Pick the curry leaves from the stalks and reserve the leaves.

Mix the ground dhal and chilli mixture with the remaining dhal, the shredded onions, the sliced green chillies, the cumin seeds, curry leaves and the salt. Thoroughly mix the ingredients together. Add some of the ground flour if the mixture is too wet.

Use about two tablespoonfuls of the mixture and press together with the palms of your hands to form a ball. The mixture will not keep its shape if the mixture is too wet. If it is too wet, add a teaspoon of flour at a time. If it is too dry the Masala Vadai pattie will crack. Prevent this by moistening with a teaspoon of water at a time.

Roll each one over the ground rice, flatten to form a patty, and set aside for deep frying. Repeat for the remaining ingredients.

Heat up the oil and when it begins to smoke, add the Masala Vadai patties. Fry till golden brown and drain on kitchen paper. Serve by itself or with fresh green chillies if preferred.

In Penang, Masala Vadai and Pisang Goreng are sold by the same vendors.

KACANG PUTEH
(Serves 6)

In the old days, there were hawkers from South India who sold Kacang Puteh, which collectively refers to the beans, nuts, pulses and other tit-bits that they offered. Some of them plied the road selling their wares while others put up their stands on the roadside, especially outside cinemas. That it what we took into the cinema before popcorn arrived. There are now few, if any, Kacang Puteh men plying the streets in Penang. I used to see one in the Pulau Tikus area, but I have not been able to find him for some time.

Kacang is 'nut' in Malay and *puteh* means 'white'. In those days if you asked for Kacang Puteh you would get the smaller variety of chickpeas – kala chana in Hindi or kondai kadalai in Tamil. Kacang Puteh has thicker and darker coloured skin compared to the larger chickpeas which we are more familiar with.

These days, the beans, nuts and pulses are toasted, boiled or fried in oil. In the old days, there were no ovens or toasters, as we know them today, so the nuts or pulses were fried in a wok with fine sand which transferred the heat to the individual nut or pulse more evenly and efficiently. When toasted, the shell of the Kacang Puteh splits open showing its yellow kernal. In those days they were sold with the skin intact but today they are sold without the skin.

The larger chickpeas could be toasted like the Kacang Puteh, fried and spiced or boiled. If you want this, you have to ask for kacang kuda (literally, horse nut). The boiled version is the subject of this recipe.

I also remember another toasted, round white bean which is not so common today. I think they were soya beans. I recall at least two types of peanuts sold by the Kacang Puteh man – one which was toasted and the other fried in oil. The toasted groundnut had its skin removed. The fried peanuts were sold with their reddish brown skins intact.

Muruku is another Indian tid-bit on sale at the Kacang Puteh stalls. In my childhood, the Muruku that we bought came in coils. Dhal, fried in oil and flavoured with salt and chillie powder, was another offering.

All the Kacang Puteh varieties were dispensed in paper cones made from pages of used school exercise books. Each cone costs 5 cents or 10 cents depending on how far your memory takes you. If you find a Kacang Puteh stall today in a shopping centre you would have to pay at least a dollar per cone.

This recipe is simple and the snack is very healthy because chickpeas have a high level of protein, fibre and minerals, especially calcium. Ground turmeric can be added to give a more distinctive yellow colour. Turmeric, by the way, has medicinal properties.

100 g chickpeas
400 ml water
⅛ tsp sodium bicarbonate
½ tsp salt
½ tsp ground turmeric, optional

Soak the chickpeas in water with the bicarbonate of soda for at least four hours. The chickpeas should nearly double in weight after they have been soaked. Drain and soak in fresh water for another 5 minutes.

Add sufficient water to more than cover the chickpeas in a pan. Add the turmeric if you wish. Bring to the boil and then turn the heat down to simmer for about 25 minutes. Add the salt and simmer for another 5 minute. Drain. The chickpeas are ready for gobbling.

KANOM JEEN NAM PRIK (SIAMESE LAKSA)

1 kati coconut milk
1 cup fresh prawn - boiled and chopped finely
1/3 cup crab meat - boiled
1/3 cup roasted peanut pounded or mashed well
1/3 cup green peas roasted and then boil until soft and pour
1/3 cup fried shredded onion)
1 cup fried shredded garlic) to be put in gravy
1 tablespoon baked and finely pounded Kha (Lengkuas)
3/4 to 1 cup sugar
1/3 cup fish sauce (Nampra)
1 ball tamarind, add 1/2 cup boiled water and squeezed
1/2 cup vegetable oil
1 teaspoon pounded, fry dried chillies

Boil coconut milk for 5 to 10 mins., and put it aside.
Put all the following into boiled coconut milk:-

1) Pounded fried chillies (according to taste)
2) 2 tablespoons pounded fried onions)
3) 2 "   "   "   garlic)
4) 1 tablespoon pounded baked Kha (Lengkuas))
5) 1 cup sugar
6) 1/3 cup fish sauce
7) Prawn, crabmeat
8) Pounded peanut   Make into past
9) Pounded mung bean (green beans)
10) Squeezed lime juice and leave the rind in

Stir until all well mixed, according to taste.
In saucepan, add 1/2 cup vegetable oil, when hot fry pounded chilli for
awhile, then put it into coconut milk with already mixed ingredients.
Stir for 1 - 2 times

les to ge with Kanom Jeen

1) Green papaya sliced finely (optional)
2) 20 cts. green winged bean, sliced fi
Chinese sweet potato leave

4 tables

THAI INFLUENCE

INDO-CHINESE, ESPECIALLY THAI, influence on Penang food is significant because it is the Thai influence that distinguishes Penang Nonya food from that of Malacca and Singapore.

Although there are very few Thais in Penang today, there was a Thai community on the island soon after Frances Light of the English East India Company arrived in Penang in 1786. They were given some land to settle in, most probably at Pulau Tikus, around Burmah Lane where the Siamese and Burmese temples are. We lived in Jones Road just behind the Burmese temple. There is a house in Jones Road where there were shows during Thai festivals. Thai influences also came through Kedah.

The best-known link between Penang and Thailand is that established by the family of Khaw Soo Cheang, later known as the Na Ranong family. Khaw arrived in Penang in 1810 from Fukien Province in China. He started as a farmer then went into trading up the coast of Southern Thailand. He left Penang six years later, diversifing into tin mining, shipping and supply of immigrant labour. Penang was an important staging post for immigration from Fujien province to the rest of Malaya and to Thailand and Indonesia. Khaw was made governor of Ranong Province by King Mongkut. Several of his sons subsequently became governors of Ranong and other adjacent Provinces in Thailand.

The Khaw had a family house in Northam Road, Penang's millionaires' row. The ground on which the Dewan Sri Pinang, the Penang State Hall stands was given by the Khaw family to the government of the day. That land was known as Ranong grounds.

Some ingredients that distinguish Thai cooking are tamarind, pepper, daun limau purut (kaffir lime leaf), daun kadok (wild pepper leaf), timun kunci (a ginger called kha chai in Thai), pea brinjal and cabai burong (literally 'bird chilli', chilli padi, a small but very hot chilli). I did not know why cabai burong is so called until I noticed birds eating the ripe chilli padi in my garden. There is a stall in the Pulau Tikus market where these herbs, spices and other ingredients like tamarind, cekur and belacan are sold.

The Burmese also influenced Penang food. The most important ingredient used in Penang cooking which originates from Burma, now Mynmar, is tanau kiam hu (salt fish). This was a product that came via Penang's entrepôt trade. Burmese guavas were also introduced to Penang. The jambu biji or jambu batu (guavas) grown in Penang when I was a child were the small and yellow variety, with more seeds than flesh; perhaps that was why it is called jambu biji as *biji* means 'seed' in Malay. Later, the Burmese *jangkong* variety was brought in. The fruits are greener, pink inside, bigger and have more flesh – more like the guava that we have today. The pear-shaped variety came in even later. My grandmother had a jangkong guava tree growing in her garden in Tanjong Tokong. I remember climbing up, swinging and falling off it.

When I was studying in London, in search of the familiar food of home before the days when Asian food and ingredients were readily available, I found a Burmese restaurant near Tottenham Court Road Underground Station which served something very close to Penang's Siamese Laksa. This Burmese Laksa, called Mohinga, is a Burmese national dish which is widely eaten for breakfast, lunch and dinner. The ingredients used, which are similar to those of Siamese Laksa, include sliced banana stem.

The serving of fresh vegetables with cooked food is a Thai practice. In both Penang Assam Laksa and Siamese Laksa Lemak, fresh vegetable condiments are also added – but with a difference – in line with Hokkien/Nonya traditions, the vegetables and pickles are finely sliced.

There are several Thai dishes which use thick rice noodles (khanom cheen in Thai), served with different curry sauces and fresh leaves and vegetables much like Laksa Lemak. Examples are Khanom Cheen Nam Prik, Khanom Cheen Nam Ya and Khanom Cheen Nam Ya Pla. Nam prik is a chilli sauce or paste like the Malay sambal hence Khanom Cheen Nam Prik has gravy made from nam prik plus ground peanuts and mung beans. Some recipes include prawns and or crabs. Khanom Cheen Nam Ya has a fish curry sauce and Khanom Cheen Nam Ya Pla has a curry sauce with fresh fish, salt fish and fermented fish sauce (nam pla). The ingredients used for these three dishes are very similar. Coconut milk, dried chillies, lemongrass, garlic, galangal and shrimp paste (belacan) are all common ingredients in the gravies.

Both the Penang Laksa and the Siamese Laksa Lemak are fish based. The *lemak* version may include prawns and/or crabs as in the Thai versions. The Thai 'Laksa' are served with fresh vegetable and, in the case of Khanom Cheen Nam Prik, vegetables fried in batter like Tempura.

There is a stall at the *kopi tiam* opposite the Pulau Tikus police station that serves both Assam Laksa and Laksa Lemak. It is run by a Thai family. I was told they have another stall at Tanjong Bungah.

While going through my mother's recipe collection I found a recipe for Kanom Jeen Nam Prik (she spelled 'cheen' as 'jeen'). That explains why my mother's Laksa Lemak is different from that cooked by my paternal aunts.

Timun kunci is also used in Hor Mok Pla (steamed fish curry) from which Penang Otak probably evolved. Hor Mok is a north-eastern Thai delicacy where the pork (Hor Mok Mu) and chicken (Hor Mok Kai) varieties are more common. There are other types of otak from other parts of Malaysia and Singapore, but the packaging used in Penang is quite distinct. Hor Mok Pla, the Thai equivalent, is steamed in a cup made of banana leaves but elsewhere, in Johor and Singapore for example, the otak is put between two coconut leaves and grilled. Penang otak is wrapped up in banana leaves, elegantly fastened together with a short length of the mid-rib of coconut fronds, and steamed. The shape is exactly the same as that of Kueh Kochi Santan, a dessert which has origins in Thailand, but it is bigger. During my younger days, when we lived with my grandmother in Macalister Road and later in Irving Road, a Thai lady went round selling Kueh Kochi Santan. She lived in Kedah Road, not far away. Kueh Kochi Santan is still available, but not everyday, in a stall at the Pulau Tikus market.

Kerabu may have originated in Thailand where there are similar salad dishes. In the Penang version, the Thai fish sauce and chillies are replaced by Sambal Belacan. There are also differences in the vegetables used. The Thais serve a greater variety of kerabu using different main ingredients which could be vegetable, fruit or meat. Likewise, there are three types of *kerabu* dishes in Penang: fruit or vegetable, with meat, and kerabu with coconut milk added.

Nasi Ulam could be classified as a kerabu. In fact, Penang style Nasi Ulam is called Nasi Kerabu in Kelantan. Nasi Ulam could be a Malay dish with Thai influence as it is more popular in the northern Malaysian states close to the Thai border, such as Kelantan, Trengganu, Perlis and Perak. Ulam is a Malay generic term for a variety of edible leaves, roots and fruits while puchok is the young leaves of plants, before they turn green. The edible ones are from the trees such as mango, cashew nut and buah petai (a bean with a strong smell which can be eaten raw as ulam).

Mee Siam is another heritage dish obviously influenced by Thai cuisine. Siam was the previous name of Thailand. Mee Siam, however, is a misnomer. There is no mee (wheat noodles) in Mee Siam. Bee hoon or thin rice vermicelli is the basic ingredient in this dish. That is because, in the Thai language, both mee and bee hoon are known as mee – ba mee and sen mee respectively. Another explanation could be that Mee Siam refers to the bee hoon used for the dish. In the Forties and Fifties, bee hoon was made locally and also imported from Thailand. The ones from Thailand were then perceived to be superior. Many Thai ingredients are used for Mee Siam like tamarind, tow chneow (fermented soya beans), coconut milk, belacan and dried shrimps. There is a very similar Thai dish, Mee Kati, which has tamarind and fermented soya beans as ingredients.

The tamarind tree is a member of the pea family. The pulp of the fruit or pod provides the sour taste to dishes like Mee Siam, Penang Laksa, Indian fish curry and Ikan Assam Pedas. Most varieties, including the Thai makahm-kaam, are more sour than sweet, but another variety from Thailand (makahm wan) is sweet and not sour at all. The word tamarind means 'date of India'. It is used in Thai and Malaysian cooking, and also by the Tamils in Sri Lanka and South India. The tamarind fruit is an irregular, curved pod of 7 to 20 centimetres. When the pods mature, the fleshy covering can be easily separated from the brittle and brown pod. It is the reddish-brown pulpy flesh inside, which covers the tamarind seeds, that are used for cooking. Tamarind is best known as an ingredient in Worcestershire sauce, a better-known brand being Lea & Perrins. In Malaysia the seeds are not eaten but used as counters in a game called Congkak.

Perut Ikan – fermented fish stomach served with fresh vegetables – is another characteristically Thai dish. Similar Thai dishes which are cooked with fermented fish sauce include Kaeng Tai Pla and Nam Phrik Pla Rhaa. In the Nonya kitchen of yesteryear, the *hu tor* or fish stomach and the roe were not thrown away when fishes were gutted and cleaned. They were washed, salted and separately accumulated in airtight bottles to ferment. After about a month, the result was used to cook Perut Ikan.

Leaves, vegetables and fruits which are grown in gardens and commonly used in Thai cuisine form the other main ingredients of Perut Ikan. They are very finely sliced in the traditional Nonya way. These include kaffir lime leaves (bai magrut), angled beans (tau phoo), long beans and a variety of brinjals, including the pea brinjal popular with the Thais. However, daun kaduk, though used in Perut Ikan, is not used in these Thai dishes.

There are two varieties of Perut Ikan in Penang – *assam* and *lemak* – with the former being more common. Both are available from a stall at the Pulau Tikus market. Bottled fish stomach can be bought at the Chowrasta Market in Penang Road and at the Balik Pulau market.

Penang otak is derived from Thai Hor Mok. Instead of being served in a cup made from banana leaves, the Penang style is wrapped into a parcel also with banana leaves.

OTAK
(Makes 16)

Steam sliced fish with a mixture of *rempah* (ground spice mix), coconut milk and egg in a banana leaf packet and you get Penang Otak – a spicy fish mousse. *Otak* means 'brain' in Malay as the texture of otak is soft, resembling brain. This sounds a bit grisly but we may be referring to prawn brains. Lengkuas (galangal) and sliced kaffir lime leaves give this *otak* a distinct flavour.

Penang Otak probably evolved from the Thai Hor Mok Pla (steamed fish curry) which is presented in a cup made from banana leaves. There are different otak from other parts of Malaysia and Singapore. These are encased in two coconut leaflets and are grilled and not steamed. For bigger portions, banana leaves are also used but the wrapping is not as elaborate as the Penang Otak parcel. For otak from the Southern states, the fish is minced and mixed with *rempah*. The otak is drier than the softer Penang version. The otak from Muar uses prawns and sotong (cuttlefish) in place of fish.

This otak recipe comes from my mother's original handwritten one which I found in her old recipe collection. She fine-tuned her recipes over the years, writing notes and making amendments. My wife used this recipe when she cooked otak to distribute to relatives. Her choice of fish was ngoh wa hu (Ikan Selangin, Threadfin) although, traditionally, the pomfret and tau theh, a larger relative of pomfret, are also used. Female gnoh wa hu are said to be better than male ones and this is reflected in the price. The males are darker, slightly grey, while the female ones are more orange.

One distinguishing feature of Penang Otak is the use of daun kadok. Kadok is a plant that belongs to the pepper family. It is related to the sireh leaves which are chewed with thinly sliced areca nut or *pinang*. It is best to use younger daun kadok which is light green.

Spice Paste

2½ tsp belacan or 2 tsp powdered belacan
20 g (about 20 medium-sized) dried chillies
40 g (about 3 medium-sized) fresh red chillies
250 g shallots
3 cm x 1 ½ cm diameter, about 20 g, kunyit (turmeric)
1 cm x 3 cm diameter, about 25 g, lengkuas (galangal)
5 cloves garlic
8 stalks serai (lemongrass)
6 pieces buah keras (candlenut)
1 tsp white pepper
3 tbsp ground rice
3 coconuts, grated, or 660 ml undiluted coconut milk

1.2 kg fish to give 750 g fillet
12 daun limau purut (kaffir lime leaves)
30 or more young daun kadok
Banana leaves
6 eggs
2 tsp salt
4 tsp sugar

Either slice the belacan thinly or fashion the belacan into a thin wafer; grill or toast till dry and slightly dark brown. Alternatively use 2 tsp of powdered belacan.

Remove the stalk and the seeds from the dried chillies and soak the chillies in water for about 15 minutes. Wash the red chillies, remove the seeds and the white ribs if you prefer your otak mildly hot; slice coarsely.

Peel the shallots, remove the root portion and slice the shallots finely. Skin the tumeric and chop the tumeric up. Clean and chop up the galangal (lengkuas). Smash the garlic, remove the skin and chop up. Remove the green portion of the lemongrass; keep only the white portion of the stalk which is approximately 5 cm from the root; smash this and slice finely.

Pound or grind the tumeric, lengkuas, lemongrass,

garlic and buah keras first, then add the belacan, dried and fresh chillies, shallots, pepper, sugar and ground rice and continue to pound or grind to get a fine paste.

Scrape or grate the coconuts if starting from the whole husked coconut. Place the grated coconut in a muslin bag and squeeze out about 660 ml of the thick, first squeeze coconut milk. Thoroughly mix about 125 ml of water to the squeezed coconut and squeeze again to obtain the second squeeze of coconut milk. Repeat with another 125 ml of water to obtain the third squeeze. You will need a total of 250 ml of second and third squeeze milk. Add the salt to the coconut milk. If concentrated coconut milk is used, mix 60 ml of the concentrated coconut milk with 250 ml of water to make up for the second and third squeeze milk.

Fillet the fish and cut into pieces of about 1 x 5 cm. Roll the kaffir lime leaves tightly and slice very thinly (about 1 mm or less). Wash the daun kadok leaves and remove the stalks. Clean the banana leaves and steam or scald in a wok of hot water to soften. Cut the leaves into rectangles about 25 cm by about 22 cm. It helps if the corners of each rectangle are cut off.

Beat the eggs and thoroughly mix the spice paste and them stir in all the coconut milk. Add the finely sliced kaffir lime leaves. Marinate the fish in this.

To wrap the otak into packets, take a piece of banana leaf and spread 2 or 3 daun kadok in the middle. Place 3 or 4 slices of fish on the daun kadok, and spoon 3 or 4 tbsp of the *rempah* over. Bring the two sides closest and furthest from you together, forming a triangular cross-section. Using your thumb and forefinger, fold the two corners on the left upwards and fold over the edges towards the centre. Repeat for the right side and seal the packet with a *lidi* or a tooth-pick.

Steam packets for 15 - 20 minutes. Serve with bread or with rice and other dishes.

HOW TO WRAP AN OTAK PACKAGE

To wrap the otak into packets, take a piece of banana leaf and spread 2 or 3 daun kadok in the middle.

Place 3 or 4 slices of fish on the daun kadok, and spoon 3 or 4 tbsp of the rempah over.

Bring the two sides closest and furtherest from you together, forming a triangular cross-section.

Using your thumb and forefinger, fold the two corners on the left upwards and fold over the edges at the centre.

Repeat for the right side and seal the packet with a lidi or a tooth-pick.

LAKSA LEMAK
SIAMESE LAKSA
(Serves 12)

Laksa Lemak or Siamese Laksa is similar to the better known Assam Laksa (see page 19) but the spicy-hot soup of Siamese laksa is lemak or creamy due to the addition of coconut milk, rather than sour. The soup is poured over rice noodles and garnished with finely shredded vegetables, blanched beansprouts, pickled leek bulb (lor keo) and pickled cucumber.

This is my mother's recipe which is different from my other aunties'. It uses pounded roasted peanuts, green mung beans, and minced prawns. I have often wondered why my mother put peanuts and mung beans into her Siamese Laksa, until I found an old recipe for Kanom Jeen Nam Prik in her recipe collection. The nam prik sauce in that dish uses pounded roasted peanuts and green beans and is both lemak, due to coconut milk, and sour, due to tamarind. My mother's recipe does not include tamarind but Laksa Lemak is served with calamansi lime (keat lah or limau kesturi) to give the dish a subtle sour flavour.

My second aunt, who is married to a Thai, uses timun kunci which gives the Siamese Laksa a nice flavor much like limau purut leaves.

In the old days, the bee hoon or laksa bor were made from scratch with rice but, these days, we can buy freshly made bee hoon or dried thick bee hoon. It is best to choose a good quality brand which does not disintegrate when boiled. When we were in London we used spaghetti, which is an acceptable substitute.

Rempah
2½ tsp belacan or 2 tsp powdered belacan
20 (about 20 g) dried chillies
8 (about 100 g) fresh chillies
225 g shallots
2 x 2 cm turmeric
2 x 3 cm lengkuas (galangal)
6 cloves garlic
2 pieces (about 3 cm each) timun kunci
5 stalks serai (lemongrass)
½ tsp white peppercorns
½ tsp black peppercorns

Soup
300 g shelled ground nuts
300 g green beans (mung beans without skin)
4 coconuts, grated or 1.6 kg grated coconut

500 g prawns
1.2 kg Ikan Kembong (Mackerel), including bones
20 daun limau purut (kaffir lime leaves)
30 daun kadok
1 cup oil (coconut oil is traditionally used)

1.5 kg fresh thick bee hoon or about ½ amount (750 g) dried thick bee hoon or equivalent spaghetti

Garnishes
250 g bean sprouts
2 cucumber
3 medium-sized onions (about 50 g each)
200 g local lettuce
100 g mint leaves
¼ pineapple
2 bunga kantan (torch ginger bud)
4 fresh chillies
12 lor keo (pickled leek bulb)
6 pickled cucumbers
10 keat lah or limau kesturi (calamansi limes)
4 tbsp heh ko (prawn paste)

Onion, bunga kantan, calamansi limes and mint leaves, some of the garnishes that make Laksa Lemak distinctive.

Either slice the belacan thinly or fashion it into a thin wafer; grill or toast till dry and slightly dark brown. Alternatively use 2 tsp of powdered belacan.

Remove the stalk and the seeds from the dried chillies and soak the chillies in water for about 15 minutes. Wash the fresh chillies, remove the seeds and the white ribs inside the chillies if you prefer your Laksa mildly hot; coarsely slice the fresh chillies.

Peel the shallots, remove the root portion and slice the shallots finely. Skin and chop the turmeric. Likewise, skin and chop up the lengkuas. Smash the garlic, remove the skin and chop up the garlic. Wash the timun kunci.

Discard the green portion of the lemongrass stalk and also the root end, keeping only the white portion which is approximately 5 cm from the root; smash the stalks and slice finely.

First pound the white and black pepper till fine then pound or grind the turmeric, lengkuas, lemongrass, garlic and buah keras into a paste and add the rest of the *rempah* ingredients, continuing to pound or grind till fine.

Fry the groundnuts until slightly brown. Skin and pound the groundnuts into a paste. Soak the green beans for at least 2 hours and boil for about 15 minutes till soft.

Grate the coconuts. Place the grated coconut in a muslin bag and squeeze out about 880 ml of thick coconut milk. Mix 200 ml of water with the grated coconut and extract the second squeeze santan. Repeat for a third and a fourth squeeze with 200 ml of water for each squeeze

Alternatively, use 880 ml of concentrated fresh coconut milk or a good brand of UHT coconut milk. Mix 80 ml of the concentrated coconut milk with 1.5 litre of water for the diluted coconut milk.

Wash the prawns, remove the heads and shells. Devein

the prawns, rinse and chop up the prawns finely. A food processor could be used. Cut the fish into a few pieces.

Boil 2 litres of water and cook the fish in it for about 10 to 15 minutes till done. Allow to cool and debone. Return the fish bones to the stock and simmer for at least half an hour to obtain a better fish stock.

Slice half of the daun limau purut finely.

Blanch the beansprouts in 1 litre of boiling water for about one minute, rinse in cold water and pour into a colander. Slice the cucumber, stack a few slices and then slice again into sticks. Slice the onions into two and slice thinly. Wash the lettuce, stack the lettuce leaves and slice them into shreds of 5 mm thickness. Separate the mint leaves from the stalk. Cut the pineapple into sticks.

Remove the outer petals of the bunga kantan and add to the fish stock. Slice the bud into two, lengthwise, and then slice thinly along the length, starting at the tip of the flower bud, till the white core is prominent.

Remove the stalks from the fresh chillies, deseed (unless you like your Laksa fiery hot) and slice diagonally. Slice the pickled leek and pickled cucumber to about 1 - 2 mm thickness. Cut the calamansi limes into two and remove the seeds.

Dilute the prawn paste with an equal volume of boiled water and set aside for serving.

Blanch the bee hoon if you are using fresh ones. If dried bee hoon is used, soak it in warm water for about ½ hour before adding a generous amount of boiling water to more than cover the bee hoon. Remove the bee hoon before the water boils. Depending on the quality, some brands of bee hoon will disintegrate if over boiled.

Heat up the wok or claypot, then add the oil. Fry the *rempah* for about 20 minutes till fragrant and the oil separates.

To this, add the fish stock, the daun kadok, both the unsliced and finely sliced daun limau purut, ground groundnuts and green beans. Bring to a boil and simmer for about 30 minutes. Pour in all the diluted second squeeze coconut milk and bring to a boil.

Add the fish and the minced prawns, bring to a boil again before lowering heat to simmer for another 10 minutes. Add the first coconut milk. Heat up the soup but turn off the heat before it boils. The hot Laksa soup now is ready to be served.

To serve, place a portion of bee hoon in a bowl, spread the garnishes on top and add the Laksa soup. Spoon on about a teaspoon of prawn paste. The juice from calamansi limes can be added if a more sour taste is preferred.

Bunga kantan or torch ginger in bud and full bloom.

KERABU

Kerabu is a Malaysian salad which consists of sliced preserved or cooked meat, fruits and vegetables – some raw, some blanched and some cooked – served with various dressings. There are as many varieties of kerabu as there are western salads.

The common dressing and garnishes used for kerabu are Sambal Belacan, Kerisik (fried grated coconut), calamasi lime and sliced shallots. Pounded dried shrimps are added especially to vegetable kerabu but not to meat or seafood kerabu. Other garnishes used selectively are coconut milk and sliced torch ginger bud (bunga kantan).

There are three main varieties of kerabu.

Vegetable or Fruit Kerabu

Besides the main vegetable or fruit ingredient for this kerabu, sliced shallot, ground dried prawns and Kerisik (fried grated coconut) are also added. Uncooked fruits like pineapple, papaya and mango, vegetables like cucumber or cabbage, and even bok nee (black wood fungus) could be used. Fruits and most vegetables are eaten raw, but some vegetables are blanched depending on preference.

One popular vegetable kerabu is Kerabu Kacang Botol. The main ingredient is kacang botol (wing beans), a hardy bean creeper that used to grow on fences or hedges in the gardens in the old days. When sliced across or diagonally the slices appear to have four wings.

Meat Kerabu

The main ingredient of meat kerabu ranges from seafood like jellyfish to animal products such as pork or chicken skin. However, if you see prawns in a kerabu, do not immediately assume that it is a prawn kerabu. This is because boiled prawns accompanies many kerabu, even the vegetable and fruit variety, including Kerabu Towgeh (beansprouts). Examples of meat kerabu are Kerabu Hai Thay (dried jellyfish), Kerabu Bak Eu Phok (fried lard), Kerabu Kerang (cockles) and Kerabu Kay Kah (skin of the chicken leg). Kerabu Bee Hoon is another typical Nonya meat kerabu because it is served with prawns. Generally, dried shrimp is not included in the ingredients if fresh prawns are used.

Kerabu with Coconut Milk Dressing

The addition of coconut milk gives this type of kerabu a slightly different flavour. Examples of this kerabu include Kerabu Kay, Kerabu Babat and Kerabu Pisang Jantung. Kerabu Kay is a Nonya hybrid name; kerabu is Malay whilst *kay* is Hokkien for 'chicken'.

Kerabu Babat uses veal tripe, beansprouts and longbeans. For Kerabu Pisang Jantung, the jantung or bud of the banana flowers is sliced and cooked with prawns.

Since Sambal Belacan (see page 39) and Kerisik (see page 184) are common to all the kerabu, they can be prepared in large quantities and stored in the refrigerator for future use.

Kerisik
Fried Grated Coconut
(Makes about 30 tbsp)

For Kerisik and grated coconut to be served fresh with desserts, only the white portion of the kernel is grated. If you have a traditional coconut grater, you would not grate down to the brown coconut shell.

It is more convenient to buy ready-grated coconut if you can, and ask for the white gratings only. You would need to be more discriminating when buying grated coconut. Some machines grate the coconut too finely. This is not suitable for Kerisik.

Kerisik is added to rendang, a dry meat curry. It also gives Nasi Ulam and kerabu that special crunchy bite if it is added just before serving. Therefore, unlike that used for rendang, Kerisik for kerabu and Nasi Ulam should not be pounded till the oil appears.

1 coconut, grated or 400 g grated coconut

Heat the wok and fry the grated coconut without oil over a medium fire till light brown. You can smell the fragrance of the toasted coconut when it is nearly ready. Stir the grated coconut continuously for about 20 minutes, especially towards the end, to ensure that the coconut is not burnt. Turn off the heat and continue to stir for about a minute or two, since the wok will remain hot.

Pound the toasted coconut in a *lesong* till fine. Do not pound too finely or oil will appear. Keep the Kerisik in a refrigerator or freezer.

Kerabu Kacang Botol
(Serves 6 with other dishes)

Kerabu Kacang Botol is a basic vegetable kerabu.

Kacang botol (wing beans or angle beans) is a hardy bean creeper. My neighbour grew some recently on our fence, co-existing with my blue butterfly pea (bunga telang, *Clitorea ternatea*).

200 gm kacang botol (angle beans)
8 (60 g) shallots
2 tbsp dried shrimp

2 tbsp Kerisik (fried grated coconut)

4 tbsp Sambal Belacan
8 - 10 keat kah or limau kesturi (calamansi lime)
2 tbsp sugar
½ tsp salt or to taste

Peel the shallots, cut off the root ends and slice the shallots longitudinally.

Soak the dried shrimps for about 10 minutes, drain and pound finely.

Slice the winged beans diagonally to 1-cm thickness. If preferred, blanch the beans in boiling water for half a minute and rinse in cold water.

Cut each calamansi lime into two, remove the seeds and squeeze out the juice. (You should get about 6 tablespoons). Dissolve the sugar and salt in the lime juice and mix in the Sambal Belacan, the winged beans, the sliced shallot and the pounded dried shrimps. Add the Kerisik and serve straight away.

Kerabu Bee Hoon
(Serves 6)

Bee Hoon, the main ingredient of this kerabu, is rice vermicelli. Kerabu Bee Hoon is a meal by itself.

300 gm bee hoon (rice vermicelli)
150 gm beansprouts
250 gm prawns
8 (60 g) shallots
3 stalks serai (lemongrass)
3 tbsp Kerisik (fried grated coconut)
12 keat lah or limau kesturi (calamanis lime)
1 torch ginger bud (bunga kantan)
2 red chillies, sliced
5 daun limau purut (kaffir lime leaves)
3 eggs
300 g tau kwa (soya bean cake)
1 tbsp sugar or to taste
1 tsp salt or to taste
3 tbsp Sambal Belacan (see page 39)
Coriander leaves

Soak the bee hoon in warm water for at least 30 minutes to separate the strands. Drain in a colander.

Bring a large pot of water to a boil and blanch the soaked bee hoon. Turn off the heat just before the water boils again. Pour the bee hoon into a colander with a pot below it to collect the hot water which is to be kept for blanching the beansprouts. Rinse the bee hoon in cold water and keep aside for serving.

Boil the hot water used for the bee hoon and use it to blanch the beansprouts. Turn off the heat just before the water boils again and drain the beansprouts in a colander. Rinse with cold water and drain again. Leave aside for serving.

Wash the prawns, remove the heads and devein. Steam or boil the prawns. Remove and cool before removing the shells.

Peel the shallots, cut off the root end and slice the shallots longitudinally.

Cut off and discard the green portion of the lemongrass stalks; keep only the white portion which is approximately 5 cm from the root. Finely slice each stalk, starting from the top and stopping short of the root end, which is a bit woody.

Cut two of the calamansi limes, remove the seeds and squeeze out the juice. Cut the remaining limes in two, remove the seeds and set aside.

Slice the bunga kantan into two lengthwise and slice crosswise thinly. Start at the tip and stop where the white core is prominent.

Put the eggs in cold water and bring to boil. Simmer for about one minute, turn off heat and leave in the hot water for at least 5 minutes. Then replace the hot water with cold water and let the eggs soak for 1 to 2 minutes. Crack and remove the shells. Slice the egg into eighths. Leave aside for garnishing.

Slice the soya bean cake horizontally into two. Heat a wok till hot and add 1 tbsp of oil. Fry the soya bean cake until just light brown. Remove and drain the oil. Cut the soya bean cake into strips of about ½ x ½ x 2 cm. Keep aside as a garnish for the kerabu.

Dissolve the sugar and salt in the lime juice. Thoroughly mix this with the Sambal Belacan, the boiled bee hoon, the blanched beansprouts, the prawns, the sliced shallot and the sliced lemongrass.

Mix in the Kerisik and garnish with the sliced torch ginger, sliced red chillies, finely sliced daun limau purut, soya bean cake and sliced egg just before serving. Offer the cut calamansi limes and Sambal Belacan on the side for diners to add to their taste.

Kerabu Kay
(Serves 6 with other dishes)

Kerabu Kay or Chicken Kerabu is a typical kerabu which uses santan or coconut milk. Interestingly, boiled prawns accompanys many such kerabu.

Cloud ear fungus (bok nee) could be added to give this dish a bit of crunch.

300 g chicken fillet
200 g prawns
6 shallots
1 stalk bunga kantan (torch ginger bud)
10 g bok nee (cloud ear fungus), optional
5 limau kesturi or keat lah (calamansi lime)
1 tbsp sugar
1 tsp salt or to taste
2 tbsp Sambal Belacan (see page 39)
2 tbsp santan or UHT concentrated coconut milk
2 tbsp Kerisik (toasted grated coconut, see page 184)

Steam the chicken. Allow it to cool and shred coarsely.

Wash the prawns, remove the heads and devein. Steam or boil the prawns. Remove and allow to cool before removing the shells.

Peel the shallots, cut off the root end and slice the shallots longitudinally.

Remove and discard the outer petals of the bunga kantan. Slice the bud into two, lengthwise, and then slice thinly along the length, starting at the tip of the flower bud till the white core is prominent. At this point, cut away the core and slice the petals.

Soak the cloud ear fungus and blanch in boiling water with a bit of salt added. Slice into thin strips of about 2 mm thickness.

Cut the calamansi limes into two, remove the seeds and squeeze out the juice.

Dissolve the sugar and salt in the calamansi juice and mix it with the Sambal Belacan, the chicken, shrimps, sliced shallot, sliced bunga kantan and bok nee.

Mix in the coconut milk, add the Kerisik and serve straight away.

Kerabu Kacang Botol

MEE SIAM
(Serves 12)

Mee Siam is a dish using bee hoon (rice vermicelli) and not – as its name implies – mee (fresh yellow noodles). In Thailand there is no distinction in name between bee hoon and mee.

The Mee Siam in this recipe is a spicy, fried bee hoon, topped with a distinctive sour and spicy gravy. There are other versions with no gravy at all or with lots of gravy; with the latter, the bee hoon may not be fried. It is important that bee hoon is not overcooked when being fried. Hence the bee hoon is divided into two portions for blanching and frying.

The spice or rempah paste is prepared first and a large portion of it is used to fry the bee hoon; the remaining is for the gravy and also for a condiment eaten with the finished dish.

I am very intrigued to find that several old Mee Siam recipes make the coconut oil from santan. More importantly, these recipes break up the light brown residue from making coconut oil and use it as a garnish. I remember the lovely fragrance very well because my mother used to make her own coconut oil when we were young. However, I don't recall her making use of the coconut oil residue.

Mee Siam can be a complete meal by itself.

500 g bee hoon (rice vermicelli)
600 g small prawns
1 tsp salt
1 litre water for prawn stock
300 g beansprouts
100 g ku chye (chives)
50 g onion, sliced
5 cloves garlic
4 tbsp tau cheo (fermented soya beans)
4 eggs
400 g tau kwa (soya bean cake)
1 tbsp oil
4 fresh green chillies, about 60 g
4 fresh red chillies, about 60 g
12 keat lah or limau kesturi (calamansi lime)

Spice Paste
5 tbsp dried prawns, about 50 g
250 g shallots
40 g dried chillies
2 tbsp belacan
2 tbsp tamarind, without seeds
200 ml water
4 tbsp oil (coconut oil is traditionally used)
6 tbsp coconut milk
1 tbsp sugar
1 tbsp salt

In the past, there were many places in Penang where soya beans were fermented to make tau cheow and soya sauce.

Soak the bee hoon in warm water for at least 30 minutes. Divide into portions to blanch separately. To blanch, boil a generous amount of water in large pot. When the water boils, add one portion of the soaked bee hoon. Turn heat off before the water boils again. Pour the bee hoon into a colander and rinse in cold water. Repeat for the other portions of the bee hoon.

Wash the prawns and remove the heads and shells, keeping them to make a stock. Devein. Slice into two if using big prawns. Marinate with 1 teaspoon of salt.

Boil 600 ml of water and add the prawn heads and shells. Bring to the boil and simmer for about 5 to 10 minutes. Keep the prawn stock aside for the gravy.

Rinse the beansprouts and remove the shells of the beans, if any. Nip off the root ends if you wish. Wash the chives and cut into lengths of about 3 cm. Boil a generous amount of water in a pot and blanch the chives for half a minute and drain in a colander. Do not overcook or the chives will loose its bright green colour. Transfer the chives into a pot of cold water and drain again. Leave aside for garnishing.

Peel the onions and cut off the root end. Cut each onion in two from top to bottom and slice finely crosswise. Skin and smash the garlic and chop finely. Mash the fermented soya beans. Divide in two portions, one for frying the bee hoon and the other for the gravy.

Put the eggs in cold water and bring to a boil. Simmer for about one minute, turn off heat and leave in the hot water for at least 5 minutes. Remove to cold water for 1 - 2 minutes. Shell the hard-boiled eggs and slice them crosswise. Leave aside for garnishing.

Slice each soya bean cake horizontally into two squares. Heat a wok till hot and add 1 tbsp of oil. Fry the soya bean cake until light brown. Drain and cut into strips of about ½ x ½ x 2 cm. Keep aside for garnishing.

Deseed the fresh chillies and slice them diagonally for garnishing. Cut the limes into two and remove seeds.

Spice Paste

Soak the dried prawns for about 10 minutes in water. Drain and pound till fine.

Peel the shallots, cut off the root ends and slice the shallots coarsely.

Remove the stalks of the dried chillies, and the seeds too if you prefer your Mee Siam mild. Soak the dried chillies in water for about 15 minute.

Either slice the belacan thinly or fashion it into a thin wafer; grill or toast till dry and slightly dark brown. Alternatively, use 4 tsp of powdered belacan.

Pound or grind the shallots, dried chillies and belacan in a food processor till a fine spice paste is obtained. About 2 - 3 tbsp of water could be added to the food processor to help the grinding process.

Soak the tamarind in about 100 ml of water. Squeeze the tamarind between finger and thumb and use a sieve to separate the pulp from the fibre. Add another 100 ml water to the pulp and repeat the process. Discard the fibre and reserve the tamarind liquid.

Heat up a wok and when it is smoking hot add 5 tbsp of oil. Fry the spice paste, stirring constantly until it is fragrant and the oil separates. Add small amounts of water if the spice paste is too dry and sticks to the wok. It could take 10 minutes or more.

Move the paste to the side of the wok and fry the 2 tbsp of pounded fermented soya beans. Add the dried prawns, sugar, salt, 200 ml water and mix thoroughly with the spice paste. Set aside half of this spice paste for frying the bee hoon. Keep three quarters of the remaining spice paste for the gravy. Use the remaining spice paste as a condiment for the Mee Siam.

Frying Mee Siam

Divide the paste and the beehoon into two equal portions to fry separately.

Heat 200 ml of water and mix with a portion of the paste, half of the beansprouts and half of the bee hoon. Stir to ensure that the chilli paste is well mixed with the bee hoon and the bee hoon is cooked. It is best to stir with a turning ladle and a pair of chopsticks. The bee hoon is ready only when it has been thoroughly mixed with the chilllie paste so that there is no white patch of beehoon in the wok. Transfer to a serving bowl.

Repeat for the other portion of the bee hoon and paste

Gravy

Heat up a wok. When it is hot, add the remaining 1 tbsp of oil. Fry the chopped garlic and sliced onions till brown, stirring continuously to ensure that they are not burnt. Add the prawns and the remaning 2 tbsps of fermented soya beans and stir. Add some water if the beans stick to the wok.

When the fermented soya beans are fragrant, add the tamarind liquid (see footnote), the prepared spice paste and the prawn stock. Bring to a boil then lower the heat and simmer for 10 minutes.

Finally, include the coconut milk and turn off the heat just before it boils again.

Serving

Spread the fried bee hoon on a large serving plate. Garnish with the chives, sliced soya bean cake, the sliced boiled eggs and sliced chillies.

Put individual portions of the fried rice vermicelli in plates and ladle the gravy over.

Offer calamansi limes to diners who prefer their Mee Siam more sour. Similarly, offer extra spice paste for those who prefer a spicier dish.

Footnote: Some tamarind are more sour than others, so you may not need to use all the tamarind liquid. Taste first.

PERUT IKAN

Perut Ikan is a Nonya seafood-based curry dish. Besides *perut ikan*, which is fish stomach in Malay, prawn is the other main seafood ingredient. Perut Ikan also contains a predominant amount of vegetables, fruits and finely sliced leaves.

There are two versions – the *assam* (sour) one and the *lemak* (coconut milk) variety. This recipe is for Assam Perut Ikan which is more common in Penang.

Most of the leaves used in Nasi Ulam are also used in Perut Ikan. In addition, other vegetables like long beans, angled beans, cucumber and brinjals are used. Besides the local brinjal which are white or purple, the tiny pea brinjal is commonly included in the dish. Pea brinjal is widely used in Thai dishes. The plant grows in many Penang gardens.

In old Nonya households, there is always an airtight bottle in the kitchen used to collect the stomach and roe of fish prepared in the kitchen. If the bottle was not properly corked, there would be the occasional explosion caused by the gas generated when the fish viscera fermented!

The fishy smell of the fermented perut ikan can be quite strong and herbs like kesom and daun limau purut are used, probably to mask the fishy smell.

The Thais use ferment fish sauce in their cooking of fish dishes like Nam Phrik Pla Rhaa and Kaeng Tai Pla. Both these dishes are accompanied by garnishes of raw vegetables and beans. The difference between these Thai fish dishes and Perut Ikan is that, for the latter, the leaf vegetables are very finely sliced and the fruits and beans are sliced and cooked.

Besides fermented fish, the common ingredients in Thai dishes and Perut Ikan are kaffir lime leaves, lemongrass, galangal, chillies, shallots and belacan.

If you cannot find perut ikan, Thai fish sauce could be used instead. You could try collecting the fish roe only, since figuring which part of the viscera to collect may not be you cup of tea! Some of my English friends are rather sqirmish about eating fish head curry, so I suspect our younger generation would not gut their own fish let alone collect the perut ikan.

You can still buy the ready-cooked Assam Perut Ikan and Lemak Perut Ikan at the Pulau Tikus market. These are very credible compared to those served in many Nonya restaurants in Penang.

Fermented perut ikan – literally, 'fish stomach.

Perut Ikan
(Serves 10 with other dishes)

100 g fermented perut ikan
350 g small prawns
2 tsp salt or to taste
1½ tbsp assam (tamarind)
2 slices assam gelugor, optional
1 tbsp sugar or to taste

Rempah
2 tsp belacan
4 dried chillies
4 fresh chillies
100 g shallots
4 x 1½ cm kunyit (turmeric)
2 x 3 cm lengkuas (galangal)
1 stalk lemongrass

Fruits & Vegetables
½ small pineapple
100 g kacang botol (angle beans)
200 g chai tau (long beans)
4 fresh red chillies
2 terong (brinjals), about 200 g
50 g pea brinjal
½ cucumber, about 150 g
5 buah belimbing, optional

Leaves & Flower
40 g daun kadok
5 daun cekur
2 daun kunyit (tumeric leaves)
10 daun limau purut (kaffir lime leaves)
10 stalks daun kesom
5 daun kuntut
1 bunga kantan (torch ginger bud)

Cabbage, optional

Thoroughly wash the perut ikan to remove the salt. Leave aside.

Shell the prawns and devein. Mix with some salt and leave aside in refrigerator.

Soak the tamarind in about 50 ml of water. Squeeze the tamarind with fingers through a sieve to separate the pulp from the fibre. Repeat with another 50 ml of water then discard the fibre.

Rempah
Either slice the belacan thinly or fashion it into a thin wafer; grill or toast till dry and slightly dark brown. Alternatively, use about 1½ tsp of powdered belacan.

Remove the stalk and the seeds from the dried chillies and soak the chillies in water for about 15 minutes. Wash the fresh red chillies, remove the seeds and the white ribs inside the chillies if you prefer your Perut Ikan mildly hot; coarsely slice the chillies.

Peel the shallots, cut away and discard the root ends and slice the shallots finely. Remove the skin from the kunyit and chop up. Clean and chop up the lengkuas. Remove the green portion of the lemongrass stalk. Use only the white portion of the stalk which is approximately 6 to 8 cm from the root; smash the stalks and slice finely. The kunyit, lengkuas and lemongrass are sliced or chopped up to make it easier to pound or grind.

First pound or grind the kunyit, lengkuas and lemongrass, then add the rest of the *rempah* ingredients and grind to a fine paste. You may have to add about 50 ml of water to ensure that the ingredients are circulating in the grinder so that the *rempah* is finely ground.

Fruits & Vegetables

Remove the skin and 'eyes' of the pineapple. Slice the pineapple into circles about 1 cm thick and then cut each slice into pieces approximately 1 x 3 cm, avoiding the core.

Cut the angle bean at a slant into 2-cm slices. Wash the long beans. Break off and discard the tips of each bean. Break each bean into lengths of about 3 cm.

Wash the fresh chillies. Cut a slit along the length of each chilli and remove the seeds. Then cut the chillies into slices of about 1.5 cm.

Cut off and discard the stalk of the brinjals and cut each brinjal into four, lengthwise. Then cut into 3-cm slices. Keep in salt water to prevent discolouration. Remove the stalks from the pea brinjals.

Cut off and discard about 3 cm of the cucumber near the stalk. Slice the cucumber lengthwise into two. Cut each half lengthwise into four if a large cucumber is used. For smaller cucumbers, cut into three lengths. Remove the core of the cucumber, then cut into 3-cm lengths.

Cut each buah belimbing into two lengthwise.

Leaves & Flower

Roll the daun kadok, cekur and daun kunyit leaves tightly together into a cylinder, using the larger leaves to enclose the smaller leaves. Then slice as finely as possible. You may wish to cut the sliced strips into shorter lengths.

Stack the daun limau purut, duan kesom and daun kentut leaves and slice thinly.

For the bunga kantan, slice each into two lengthwise and slice finely from the tip of the flower till the white core becomes apparent.

Assembly

Mix about 100 ml of water to the *rempah* and boil it in an anodized wok or a clay pot for about 10 minutes. (An anodized wok is used because tamarind is acidic.) Add about 2 tbsp of water if the *rempah* is too dry or whenever it sticks to the wok or pot.

Add 1.5 litres of water, the tamarind juice and the perut ikan. Bring to boil and simmer for about 20 minutes.

Add the fruit and vegetable ingredients. Bring to the boil and simmer for about 10 minutes. Assam gelugor could be added if you like your Perut Ikan to be more sour.

Add the prawns, salt and simmer for about 5 minutes. The sugar may not be required since the pineapple should give the dish sufficient sweetness, so add sugar according to taste.

Finally, add the finely sliced leaves and bunga kantan, bring to boil and turn off the heat. The vegetables will turn black if over boiled. Spread out the sliced vegetables; make sure they are not clumped together.

Serve with rice and other dishes.

Buah belimbing (front) and pea brinjal.

ACKNOWLEDEGMENTS

A book like this would not have been possible without the help from a large number of relatives and friends. I would like to acknowledge the influences of my late mother, Khoo Chiew Kin, and my late father, Ong Kim Hoon who provided the right environment years ago that made this book possible. Most of the old family photos in this book were taken by my father. My mother was the one who let us loose in the kitchen at an early age, after she realized that my paternal uncles could cook. In writing this book, I have relied on the many written versions of recipes that were prepared by members of my family – my mother, father and sisters.

I would like to thank, in particular:
My wife, who fine-tuned and specializes in some of the recipes; she can wrap otak better than anyone I know;

My brothers, Jin and Leong, and sisters, Inn and Ai, whom I often asked about the food that we ate as we grew up;

Cousin, Sandy, who explained how many dishes were cooked by my *tua kor* (eldest aunt) and how Sandy does it today;

My wife's *jee chim* (second aunt), Mdm Lim Say Choo, who taught us to make some lost heritage dishes and gave invaluable tips;

My wife's *sar kim* (third aunt), Mdm Phuah Kim Geok, who went into details of some recipes;

Cousin, Letticia, who explained some cooking techniques and helped me understand the difference between Penang and Singapore cooking;

Jin and cousin, Yoong, who commented on my early drafts;

Cousin, Chai, who provided some explanations about Thai food;

Nooi Kim, who occasionally sent me her recipes;

Maureen and Laurence, for contributing family photographs;

My children, Clara, Mark and Kim from whom I learned (to me) some of the not so obvious mistakes that can be made in cooking – a teacher learning from his students; and

The Scouts, for the excellent training I received in the movement.

I sought advice, but the final decision as to what goes into this book is mine and mine alone. Invariably, my recipes are different from those of other families. This is inevitable because different families have their variations of even classic dishes, often due to family preferences. There are variations to recipes even among my aunties, not to mention the in-laws from my father's side! When the same dish is cooked by my cousins, each of them produced some variations. Also, as we grow older our memories are not as good. In this respect, I have had some disagreement with my brother, Jin. I asked him why a specific ingredient was missing in a dish and he in insisted that that was how it should be – until I consulted our mother's recipe.

Published by
Landmark Books Pte Ltd
5001 Beach Road
#02-73/74
Singapore 199588

https://www.facebook.com/groups/PenangHeritageFood/

First published 2010. Reprinted 2012 and 2015.

ISBN 978-981-4189-61-3
Printed in Malaysia